PARTNERSHIPS
CONNECTING
SCHOOL AND
COMMUNITY

By Anne C. Lewis

Edited by T. Susan Hill
and Debbie Demmon-Berger

Ministry of Education, Ontario
Information Services & Resources Unit,
13th Floor, Mowat Block, Queen's Park,
Toronto M7A 1L2

Published by the American Association
of School Administrators
1801 N. Moore Street
Arlington, Virginia 22209-9988

OTHER PUBLICATIONS on school-community partnerships available from AASA

Parents . . . Partners in Education (booklet and video program)
Los Padres . . . Participantes En La Educación
Business and Industry . . . Partners in Education
Citizens and the Schools . . . Partners in Education
Partnerships
Building Public Confidence in Our Schools
Holding Effective Board Meetings
Skills for Successful School Leaders
Excellence in Our Schools . . . Making It Happen
Public Relations for Administrators
Public Education . . . A Sound Investment in America (video program)
The Race We Dare Not Lose (slide-tape program)
A Theme for Your Schools . . . Why and How
Building Morale . . . Motivating Staff

Additional copies of these publications and others may be ordered from AASA Publications, 1801 N. Moore St., Arlington, Virginia 22209-9988; (703) 875-0730 or 528-0700. Price lists and catalogs are available on request.

Partnerships . . . Connecting School and Community, Copyright 1986, American Association of School Administrators, Arlington, Virginia.

Design by The BUSINESS SERVICE NETWORK, Ijamsville, Maryland

Library of Congress Card Catalog No.: 071943
ISBN: 0-87652-102-2
AASA Stock Number: 021-00182

Points of view or opinions expressed in this book are those of the authors and do not necessarily represent the official position of AASA.

(AASA is an Equal Opportunity Employer.)

Table of contents

Foreword 7

Overview
Schools have long benefited from parent and business volunteers; today, those volunteer efforts are being marshalled in a big new way. Here's what's happening, and why 9

Chapter 1: National momentum
Examples abound of successful partnerships between schools and the nation's corporate giants, national civic, and public interest groups 17

Chapter 2: State leadership
Governors and corporate CEOs likewise have spawned a multitude of inventive ways to invest private resources in public schools 29

Chapter 3: Local initiatives
In building coalitions, rural and small districts continue to find one another their own best partners; urban and suburban districts, meanwhile, find their schools working with local businesses, civic groups, and others 37

Chapter 4: Additional partners
Also finding benefits for themselves in school partnerships are institutions of higher education, foundations, and individuals 55

Chapter 5: Lessons learned from partners
Mutual benefits. Clear focus. Open channels of communication. Strong partnerships share these and other traits. Here's how to duplicate their success in your community 69

Exhibits 91

Acknowledgments 125

A definition

A cooperative endeavor between a school or school district and a corporation, business, civic organization, college or university, foundation, governmental agency, or other entity where a formal arrangement is made to share resources (including human, material, or financial) with the ultimate objective of promoting the interests of the schools. From "Partnerships in Education: Trends of the Future," U.S. Department of Education Survey.

Foreword

Even two years ago, when this book was a mere idea, the evidence already was mounting: A new, mutually beneficial kind of partnership was forming between private enterprises and public schools. No longer were schools asking for contributions from local businesses, simply hoping that the tax benefits of such gifts made the gesture worthwhile.

Instead, in one town, a computer company donated hardware for a high school computer lab, and then the school let its benefactor use the lab for staff training in the evenings and on weekends.

Elsewhere, a corporation funded training for local teachers who wanted to make and repurpose videodiscs for classroom use. In return, the teachers collaborated with their business partner, after school hours, to produce videodiscs for corporate training.

Several corporate giants regularly win free publicity in the national media for sponsoring school contests that encourage children to read, recognize teacher excellence, fund scholarships, and more.

Equal partners in a joint venture—that's the spirit of today's partnerships, although philanthropic gifts do not appear to have gone out of style.

To wit: After 30 years, businesses and charitable foundations in Cleveland are still sending needy students through college, providing them with summer jobs, and helping them find work after graduation. Recently, one citizen in a small Kentucky town singlehandedly raised $200,000 for local school projects. For seven years, New York City's top education, corporate, civic, and community leaders have donated their time to developing ways higher education institutions can help public education.

School systems are partnering up to provide services that one system could not afford alone. With the advent of technology, small districts everywhere seem to be banding together, pooling resources for hardware acquisition and sharing teachers over the microwave transmissions of public television. In Texas, a consortium of mostly large districts is developing a $3 million courseware package using $75,000 in seed money from each member.

With examples like these, is there any wonder why a book on partnerships —packed with tips for success, complete with ideas for school districts of all demographic configurations—seemed like a good idea? Partnerships are helping to revitalize schools everywhere.

We set out to find more, surveying AASA members, searching the literature, interviewing school partners as we found them. The result is this book, which is designed to help schools become even more effective.

During 1985-86, several national groups have reported on the dire consequences to the nation if its public schools do not better prepare today's students for life in the high-tech, global economy of the 21st century. Without exception, they call for a marshalling of private resources to help a system that cannot expect significant increases in public funds. "Private enterprise for the public good" is what task force

Partnerships

members call the effort they hope to summon—but they describe partnerships, pure and simple.

In the pages that follow, we'll show you partnerships whose members come from every imaginable walk of American life and whose activities are as diverse as the thousands of schools in which they occur. Today, at this moment, people are helping their schools—on local, state, and national levels; in businesses, in professional and civic groups, and in foundation and university offices.

Perhaps this effort, magnified tenfold or more, can indeed infuse our schools with the resources required to meet the great challenges before them. At the very least, partnerships offer private individuals, organizations, and businesses a unique means for buying into the future of their public schools.

Whatever your plan for partnerships between your school and community, we hope this book serves as a practical and valuable guide.

>
> Richard D. Miller
> Executive Director
> American Association
> of School Administrators

Overview

Question: Altogether, in the nation's more than 15,000 public school districts, how many gifts of time, material, or money are donated by outside individuals or groups in any one year? Hint: Exclude from your answer all traditional, volunteer PTA and booster club activities, along with work training programs, valuable as they are.

If your answer is somewhere in the neighborhood of 46,000 annual contributions, you're right on target, according to the most recent statistics on the subject. Conducted in 1984—the year designated by President Ronald Reagan as the National Year of Partnerships in Education—a U.S. Education Department survey found 46,338 different kinds of partnerships in operation among the 56 percent of school districts who responded to the survey.

The largest number of projects was sponsored by businesses and included donations of equipment and materials, special awards for students and teachers, corporate staff time for guest lectures, and so on. (Foundations proved to be the least common type of school sponsor.) More than two-thirds of responding districts reported a substantial increase in their partnership efforts in recent years; the greatest gains were made by large districts (more than 25,000 students) in the northeast region of the country.

In another recent quantitative analysis of partnerships, Paul Barton, president of the National Institute for Work and Learning in Washington, D.C., found 300,000 to 400,000 business people serving on school advisory committees on vocational education.

"There is, out there, a lot of experience to weigh, and for those interested in doing so, to build on," observes Barton.

According to two other studies of school partnerships, American businesses give as little as $13 million or as much as $50 million to schools each year. Says Dale Mann, the Columbia University Teachers College professor who conducted one of the studies, "Clearly the dollar value of the goods and services received may be less significant than the possibility that mutual understanding may mature into political collaboration and, thus, more adequate financial support for the schools."

More than numbers. Despite Barton's and Mann's hints that there might be more to the story, the sheer number of partnerships and their diversity comprised the "big story" at the first National Symposium on Partnerships in Education in 1984. Only a year later, however, it was the dramatic change in the tone of school partnerships that symposium speakers drove home.

The breadth and depth of voluntary contributions, they said, were markedly greater than ever before in public school history.

The reason?

"Altruism no longer appeared to be the sole motivation for business contributions to schools," observes Michael Timpane, president of Columbia University Teachers College. "Rather, business and education had discovered a new strong common ground—mutual self-interest."

Partnerships

For the first half of this century, a school's most loyal "outsiders" had been parents and other civic-minded school volunteers. Local businesses—the other major contributor—primarily gave to the schools a few of their fellows, as school board members.

With the major social upheavals that followed World War II, the involvement of the loyal "outsiders" waned. Many women gave up volunteer efforts to enter the workforce, and the pool of businessmen willing to accept school board service—often a stage for societal controversies—dwindled.

Busy in their own changing world, school personnel generally did not reach out to stop their going—although in some locales the demands made on school leadership by organized and vocal factions within communities continued to give interested citizens structured, meaningful roles in the schools.

Partners need mutual understanding

Schools and business can benefit greatly from partnerships, but establishing a basis for mutual understanding takes work.

The point is illustrated by researcher Dale Mann, who studied urban partnerships for the Exxon Education Foundation: "An urban superintendent lamented that he could never convince the business community that the schools needed more money, not just money-saving measures. Finally a leading accounting firm offered to review the school system's audit practices. 'As a result, business now believes us if we say we're broke,' the superintendent told me."

Such misunderstandings abound, in both the education and business worlds, according to a task force created by the Education Commission of the States under former North Carolina Governor James Hunt. Among the most common:

- Some business people believe they pay for education twice, first through taxes, then by sponsoring remedial programs for employees; they also harbor a belief that at least some educators want assistance to make up for lost public funds.
- Some educators believe that business is narrowly profit-motivated, and that business people underestimate the significant commitment of people, time, and money that improving education requires.

These differences have to be overcome and partnerships are a way to do that, says Columbia University Teachers College President Michael Timpane. "Good projects break down stereotypes about the schools and bring hundreds of people into the schools."

Overview

It was not until the mid-1970s, when test scores started falling, discipline problems moved to the top of the public's list of what's most wrong with American schools, and both employers and colleges began to complain that high school graduates could not perform tasks requiring basic skills, that the quality of public education again found a high place on outsiders' agendas.

Along with a barrage of criticism and suggestions for improvement, schools found themselves deluged with helpful volunteers. This time around, however, businesses and community groups reached out with something new—planned, organized efforts for long-term school/community commitments. Further, state and national groups began organizing local efforts.

Thus, in Houston, a local utility company lent its engineers and accounting personnel to school staff members who wanted a few quick math lessons before taking the state-mandated math proficiency examination. And, on the national scene, the U.S. Chamber of Commerce launched a series of ten regional workshops on business involvement in schools, produced eight hour-long specials on education for its cable television program, and published a comprehensive resource book, *Business and Education: Partners for the Future.*

Other evidence mounted that partnerships in education were being formed at all levels with all kinds of groups:

- The Monsanto Corporation, headquartered in Springfield, Massachusetts, opened its doors to local teachers for day-long seminars on scientific advances.
- Kiwanis Club members in Fort Worth, Texas, trained to be "special friends" to primary children who, in teachers' judgments, appeared high risks for educational failure.
- American Airlines raised $500,000 for the Chicago schools by donating one dollar of each ticket sold in Chicago over a four-month period.

Here and there, private groups and individuals contributed in a groundswell of activity that by 1985 made private contributions to public schools "one of the most significant connections in American education," says Timpane.

The business connection. To appreciate the revival of business's commitment to the schools, we must look to the past and toward the future, say many school observers. They note that history tells us why businesses periodically become involved in schools, while economic forecasts contain the reasons for their renewed interest today.

"From a historical perspective, school/business relationships appear somewhat cyclical," says Marsha Levine, education consultant for the American Enterprise Institute (AEI). Industry's need for trained workers determines its degree of involvement with the schools, she says.

Columbia's Timpane agrees, noting that business interest in public schools was "pervasive" through 1950. Not only were most board members from the business community, but many administrators modeled their management styles on business practices.

"Business leaders and educators readily agreed that an important

Partnerships

objective of education was the preparation of students for a productive work life," says Timpane. From that "comfortable consensus," developed all school curricula, testing, placement, and counseling programs.

"The prodigious expansion of the public schools after the Second World War turned out to be the last page of this chapter in the history of business involvement in the schools," Timpane notes in a *Phi Delta Kappan* article (February 1984).

Throughout the 1960s and early '70s, business interest in public education dwindled, first because an abundant force of qualified workers materialized as the "baby boomers" grew up, and second because a horde of other players took to the school field—the courts, parent advocates, state and federal legislators.

Business interests were quickly eclipsed.

Today, economic pressures have generated a vast new period of business involvement because, say corporate leaders, schools could do a far better job teaching the country's future workforce how to use the modern technological advances upon which our future economic prosperity will be based.

Urgent then and now

"We should act at once because of the stress of foreign competition. We are 25 years behind most of the nations that we recognize as competitors. We must come nearer to the level of international competition. As every establishment must have first-class mechanical equipment and management, so must it have in its workmen skill equal to that of competitors, domestic or foreign. The native ability, the intuitive insight, courage, and resourcefulness of American workmen is quite unsurpassed.... It is their misfortune that they have not been given by this country that measure of technical instruction that is their due, and are by no means equal in technical skills to the workers of continental Europe...."
National Association of Manufacturers, 1905

"Three years ago, the country was in the grip of the most severe recession since the Great Depression. While most Americans were deeply concerned about our economic prospects, and were persuaded that the economy could not prosper as long as the quality of education continued to decline, few perceived that the world economy was in the midst of a profound transformation, one that demands a new understanding of the education standards necessary to create the kind of high-wage work force that can compete in a global economy."
Carnegie Forum on Education and the Economy, 1986

Overview

"We're hurtling into the future at such speed that we're likely not to be ready for it," columnist Jack Anderson told educators at a 1986 meeting for technology users. He and others regularly rattle off statistics to prove the point:
- Seventy-five percent of all children entering school this fall will enter the job market in jobs that do not exist today.
- Most of those jobs will involve technology.
- Other nations are doing a better job preparing their children for this tomorrow. In fact the U.S. usually ranks **last** in most studies comparing education in the top 12 industrial nations.

"We haven't prepared our kids to be sovereigns, to take over," says Anderson. "We haven't taught them that with democracy comes responsibility, not just privilege."

Anderson, along with many business leaders, is clearly appalled by statistics that show 70 percent of all German, Japanese, and Russian high school graduates are highly proficient in science and math, while less than six percent of U.S. students have achieved those levels of proficiency.

"Clearly, we have got to prepare our young people for math and science careers if this nation is to regain its competitive position in the world economy," says Anderson.

For these reasons, the business interest in schools has advanced on all fronts. Locally, individual schools have "adoptive" businesses and corporations, and chambers of commerce pursue deliberate efforts to link up with schools. At the state level, education reform task forces are led by business leaders and their influence frequently becomes the strongest ally schools have in securing greater financial support for reforms. Nationally, chief executive officers lend their expertise to important studies, and major corporations fund projects and commit corporate leadership down through the ranks to collaborate with schools.

Says researcher Levine, "Structural changes in the economy have underscored the relationship between education and economic growth and enhanced the view that education is an investment in human resource development."

The broader society connection. The fact that business leaders are becoming the strongest allies of school reforms has not diminished the impact of other groups. Instead, it is looked on as a means of achieving what everybody wants—better schools.

"We must create a shared approach to education," argues David Seeley, author of *Education Through Partnership*. Says Seeley, who for many years directed one of the earliest coalitions supporting schools, the New York Public Education Association, "Genuine reform depends on working on relationships—with the home, community groups, politicians, and businesses."

Where education is a community enterprise, results have been encouraging, Seeley says, in a study he conducted of home-school-community partnerships for the Charles Stewart Mott Foundation.

Such partnerships are a natural outgrowth of the extra tasks society

Partnerships

National task forces call for partners

"Children do not just grow up," writes U.S. Secretary William Bennett in *First Lessons,* his 1986 report on the state of American elementary education. "They must be raised by the community of adults—all adults."

Only if the total community accepts "as its solemn responsibility—as a covenant—the nurture, care, and education of the coming generation" will elementary schools fulfill their potential, says Bennett.

The secretary's report is one of many published since the early 1980s, when the so-called excellence movement was launched by "a sweeping reassessment of the basis of the nation's economic strength and an outpouring of concern for the quality of American education," as one report puts it.

All suggest that deep public commitment to the schools—manifested in partnerships above and beyond formal school/community relations—is the most viable means of improving public education. A sampling from recent reports:

● Improving the quality of education is not a cost, but "the most important investment this nation can make," says the 1985 report from the Committee for Economic Development, *Investing in Our Children.* The CED, whose membership consists of 200 chief executive officers and university presidents, pledged the support of business leadership, from the grassroots up, to school improvements suggested in its report.

● "Those who would reform from the outside and those who would do so from the inside [must] make common cause," says the 1986 Carnegie Forum report, *A Nation Prepared.* The report suggests reforms that would reassert the "the primacy of education as the foundation of economic growth."

● If schools are to improve, says *Time for Results,* the 1986 National Governors Association report on education, the "wider public" must be involved—not merely to gain new ideas, but more important "to tap and focus energy and commitment."

"These reports put everyone on the hook: parents, other citizens, business people, the media, school administrators, teachers, school boards, governors, and state legislators," says Richard Miller, AASA executive director. "That is healthy, because the schools can't do it alone. To be as successful as possible, everyone must be a part of the educational team."

Overview

today asks its schools to perform, says researcher Levine. "As the definition of education expands beyond traditional schooling—to include the lifelong influences of home, workplace, church, and community—it carries with it implications for shared institutional responsibilities." It is shared responsibilities that will make school reforms succeed because, as Seeley puts it, the widespread demand for improved achievement encourages schools to shift from a "service delivery" to a "performance outcome" approach to education.

Other indicators that partnerships may indeed help reforms succeed are these, according to Timpane and Seeley:

- The idea of partnerships started at the grassroots level, with simple career days, and has moved on to corporate job guarantees for graduates and business-sponsored public relations campaigns for schools. "When projects move from the periphery to the center, they have more chance of succeeding," says Timpane.
- Partnerships have moved from the project to the policy-making level. "True improvement takes place at the policy level," says Timpane, who adds that policy-making sanctions the public's will about its schools.
- Policy interests have gone from narrow to broad perspectives, from an emphasis on vocational skills for students, for instance, to an emphasis on improving the professional environment of the teaching profession. "Business people have looked at this issue from the standpoint of employers and realized that the work environment for teachers needs to change if schools are to get and keep good people," says Timpane.
- Policy issues have gone quickly to the state level, as the federal government has tried to relinquish interest in local programs and governors have stepped in to coordinate reforms. "State governors can mobilize support for educational partnerships in ways that local school officials would find difficult," says Seeley.

In the chapters that follow, we'll look at successful partnerships at the local, state, and national levels to see what partners say makes their projects work.

Chapter 1

National momentum

It's hard to pinpoint the precise moment when the grassroots generation of school partnerships reached critical mass and exploded into a national movement. Yet today, when public schools are the topic, a sense of national purpose lights eyes from the nation's political capital in Washington to its commercial center in New York, and thence ripples out across the country.

Rededicating themselves to helping schools are such corporate giants as Pizza Hut and the Dupont Co., such civic leaders as the U.S. Chamber of Commerce, and a plethora of nonprofit groups with national agendas for the schools.

The U.S. Postal Service—a resource available to every school community—has set up Postal Resources for Educational Partnerships, which provides speakers, student counseling on study skills and drug abuse, science fairs, and field trips.

Even Uncle Sam has reached out from federal agency offices and military bases.

In Boulder, Colorado, since 1979 staff from the National Bureau of Standards (NBS) have taught science and math lessons to students in grades 4 to 12 and created special science videotapes and kits for their regular classroom teachers. Continental drift, lasers, cryogenics: All are included among the dozens of subjects covered in NBS's Career Awareness and Resource Education Program. The program also provides for students to tour NBS headquarters, receive career counseling, and "shadow" staff whose jobs students find intriguing.

From coast to coast, the U.S. armed services sponsor science fairs, tutor students, staff booths on career day, and offer vocational counseling. In San Diego, California, where the U.S. Navy is the city's second largest industry, officers and enlisted men have found that adopting public schools can lead to their own personal adoption by thankful students who invite their new family members home for holiday dinners.

Here is the Navy's own story—and others—as told by national leaders in the partnership movement:

U.S. Navy: San Diego's second largest industry recruits officers and enlisted men to take handicapped students to concerts . . . .

Among the myriad partnerships between the San Diego public schools and the city's second largest employer are these eight stories:

Partnerships

- When the USS Ajax adopted San Diego's Tierrasanta Elementary School, one crew member volunteered to be a pen pal with students in each classroom in the school. Students and crew exchange letters when the ship's at sea; when it docks, students tour the ship and learn that navy life offers a variety of careers. The ship, for instance, has its own photographers who love to give aspiring student camera-buffs a few tips on film development in the ship's own darkroom. Once, ship illustrators designed artwork for the school's media center. So warmly received are the crew's attentions that students regularly invite their pen pals home for holiday meals.
- Every week, officers and enlisted men from the Naval Air Station (Miramar) visit the classrooms at Hickman Elementary School, offering their services as tutors. One serviceman goes every day.
- Students should have tangible incentives for achievement. With this thought in mind, the servicemen at the Naval Oceans Systems Center now award students at Gompers Secondary School for academic excellence by hiring 12 of them each summer to work one-on-one with center researchers and scientists.
- Pacific Beach Junior High School had no computer, a void remedied by the Naval Personnel Research and Development Center. Center staff not only bought and installed a computer and 11 terminals, but also sent three data processing people to the school—every day—to help teachers become computer literate.
- A teaching facility itself, the Service School Command saw itself as a natural resource for teachers at Kearny High School who wanted to learn how to use computers for individualized instruction. Command staff have now passed on their training techniques to their public school colleagues.
- When Henry High School needed stadium lights, the crew aboard the USS Denver held "anchor pools" and raised more than $1,800 toward the purchase.
- Mental and physical sports are the gift of the Fleet Command Training Center (Pacific) to Silver Gate Elementary School. Center staff first set up an after-school computer club; now Navy personnel staff a sports clinic one day a week, taking students through their paces in volleyball or kickball games and on an obstacle course.
- Handicapped children receive special attention from the U.S. Navy Surface Warfare Officers School. In adopting the Schweitzer School, Navy personnel found themselves surrounded by students clamoring for help to go places and do things they normally could not. Now concerts and fairs in the city park, museum trips, and visits to the local art galleries are within every student's reach, as their Navy partners lend a helping hand. For a science fair, where botany projects were the order of the day, the Navy staff built waist-high planter boxes so wheelchair-bound students could participate.

For more information on military partners, contact any armed forces recruiting office. The National Association of Secondary School Principals also has guidelines, useful to both military and school personnel, on partnerships between the two groups.

U.S. Chamber of Commerce: How one group shook the national apathy toward educational quality....

More than 20 years ago, the U.S. Chamber of Commerce took a long look at how schools and businesses might help one another more. But between then and 1980, the Chamber—like many groups—entered a period of complacency about the public schools.

"There was a time of national apathy toward educational quality," says Robert Martin, the Chamber's associate manager of resource policy and author of a book that marked the Chamber's return to active involvement in school progress.

Publishing Martin's *Business and Education: Partners for the Future* was but one indicator of the national Chamber's commitment to reforge links between schools and business. In the early 1980s, the Chamber also conducted ten national workshops on the subject and produced eight hour-long television specials.

Explaining the Chamber's motivation, James Campbell, then chairman of the organization's education, training, and employment committee, said: "Small business firms—those with fewer than 100 employees—dominate Chamber membership; 80 percent of our 200,000 members are with small businesses. Seven of eight of these firms' employees come from the public schools, and 70 percent of all first jobs held by high school graduates are in small businesses."

By 1995, predicts Campbell, 80 percent of all new jobs will be in small businesses.

The natural link between small businesses and schools, then, is clear, but if it needs to be underscored, there's this fact, says Campbell: "Only 2,000 of the country's more than 15,000 school districts have resident Fortune 500 companies; the rest rely on small businesses for economic prosperity."

What the Chamber suggests is that people on the boards of local chambers sit down with the local school board and superintendent and talk about the strengths and weaknesses of the school system.

"I guarantee that business people will not know what they need to know about local schools," says Campbell, "but they are more anxious than ever to become an ally—if you just reach out."

When local chamber/school partnerships succeed, it's because both groups have talked "in plain language" about what each other needs and "the reaching out is mutual," Campbell says. It also is helpful if both groups assess community resources and "don't reach beyond them;" write down everything on the mutual agenda; and tie projects to deadlines.

Since the Chamber recognizes that what local schools need most is help in the political arena, it is urging business people to run for school board office, as they used to do.

"Business people are not educators," concludes Campbell, "but their ideas are transferable."

Partnerships

Working with coalitions

People tend to band together when a common threat or opportunity arises. This is what coalitions are all about. A coalition is a group of organizations or individuals, often with diverse interests, formed to deal with a common issue or to achieve a common purpose.

A school district can help start coalitions. Bringing groups together to focus on issues increases understanding and support. Forming a coalition requires planning. Here are some of the steps in the process.

- Explore the issues. The issue might be getting education back on the community agenda, or the issue might be more specific, such as extending the school year.
- Identify groups—business leaders, nonparents, and/or others—that have a stake in the issue.
- Convene a meeting. State the coalition's purpose as you see it.
- Select a chairperson. The leader might or might not be someone directly involved in the issue. However, the chairperson must be someone with the time, energy, ability, and commitment to do the job.
- Work together as a team, become informed, and deal with the issue. Here are some guidelines for setting up successful coalitions:

—Select members who will work not out of self-interest but out of concern for the common good.
—Be sure members have the information they need to make wise decisions and encourage them to develop strategies to deal with the issues.
—Be positive and look to the future.
—Keep coalition members, and your staff, board, and community informed through a communications network.
—Avoid voting; work on the basis of consensus.
—Don't insist that all groups deal with objectives in the same manner. Try to agree on general ideas and projects.
—Be willing to make compromises for the common good. Be a good negotiator.

Coalitions dealing with issues concerning education are a natural part of the school and public relations program. By bringing together unique individuals and groups to work on a common concern, schools can turn diversity into unity that creates a consensus for education.

From Public Relations for Administrators, *published by the American Association of School Administrators, 1985.*

National momentum

California Chamber of Commerce: This state got the national message—and ran....

When the "get involved" message went out from the U.S. Chamber of Commerce, the California chapter was challenged. In January 1984, Project BET (Business and Education Together) launched six pilot programs that placed state chamber staff right at school sites. More than 30 guides were published that year and distributed to 80 local chambers, who in turn launched their own school/business partnerships.

The proceeds of those efforts:
- In Huntington Beach, the chamber's annual golf tournament turned into a fundraiser that pays out five scholarships to business-oriented students. Every year, the chamber also sponsors an outstanding teacher of the year award in each high school.
- In Rancho Bernardo, high-achieving students are given discounts in cooperating local business establishments.
- The Madera chamber regularly sponsors a half-day for business people to visit classrooms and a half-day for teachers to visit businesses.
- The Business-Education Exchange in Walnut Creek pairs 75 students with area businesses for an indepth day of "shadowing" employers.
- Students get experience at job interviews in La Habra when chamber volunteers (working with school counselors) conduct mock interviews; the videotaped sessions are critiqued by the counselor, interviewer, and student.
- In Pico Rivera, the chamber, city council, and school district all worked together to produce telephone books with pictures so children might find emergency numbers fast. The results: *Tele-Photo Phone Book* and *Emergency Phone Book for Kids*.
- Youth counseling was the goal of the Van Nuys chamber's "Youth Resource Unit." Part of an anti-gang project, the project runs full time on the high school campus.

Chevron Corporation: A benevolent giant funds science, music, history, and more....

Bill Moyers would not be taking his Emmy Award-winning walk through the 20th century if the Chevron Corporation were not committed to public education.

"Our programs for the most part mix community service with a benefit for the corporation," says Barbara Bontemps, Chevron's director of educational programs, "although there are exceptions."

In fact, there are many exceptions. A relatively small one is the Chevron School Broadcast, which recently produced a series of 15-minute radio programs celebrating jazz. More to the point is Chevron's annual donation of $8.5 million to various scholarship and fellowship programs at colleges and universities. Further, the company donates about $4 million each year to "precollegiate partners."

In addition, company personnel at various sites work with local

Partnerships

schools on their own projects. A Chevron geologist, for instance, invites elementary school children from the La Habra, California, schools along on his fossil digs.

Similar small and large science education projects are what Chevron thinks will ultimately benefit the corporation—which is the reason Chevron funded SCOPE. The goal of the Science Cooperative for Outstanding Public Education is to improve science instruction in San Luis Obispo, California, schools. A predominantly rural area, still maintaining some two-room schools, San Luis Obispo lacked funds but not imagination.

"What attracted us to the project," says Bontemps, "was the thoroughness of the planning and the potential for long-range success."

Among SCOPE's activities are these:
- Creating a network of people from all of the county's schools, its higher education campuses, and teacher education and computer center.
- Letting those people develop an overall plan for science education.
- Developing a 220-page science curriculum prototype and acquainting teachers with it in a series of summer workshops.
- Developing a companion directory of local science resources.

Teachers also attended a forum to learn about Chevron's Energy 80 curriculum series, visited an offshore oil platform, attended a marine biology seminar, and went on a two-day tour of Bay Area science resources—all at company expense.

Corporate America: Student achievers in reading, chemistry, business win jobs, scholarships....

"What concerns me is the economic cost to our nation of the wasted talents of millions of people eager, but unable or untrained, to work. This amounts to an enormous squandering of our human capital. We must reverse our declining support for education," says Time Inc. President Dick Munro.

That sentiment apparently has echoed in corporate offices across America and, as these examples show, support for education is growing once again:

Honeywell. "Although technological and business-oriented disciplines are natural avenues for Honeywell to explore, we are committed to supporting and facilitating educational endeavors—whatever the field—that serve a community need in a unique way," proclaims Honeywell in its *Community Responsibility Report.*

The company backs those words with considerable action, funding scholarships and research, rehabilitating facilities to accommodate wheelchairs, and giving time and money to help minorities enter technological and business fields. Students can attend Honeywell seminars and laboratories to "upgrade their readiness ... to pursue technological education," the report notes.

National momentum

Pizza Hut. "Pizza" is a word that has almost instant recognition among young people, even those just learning to read. It has become more closely identified with reading in an unusual project called BOOK IT!, sponsored by Pizza Hut Inc.

BOOK IT!, a national reading incentive program for students in grades 1 to 6, recognizes and rewards students for reading achievement at five different levels. Teachers set individual monthly extracurricular reading goals according to each participating child's ability and reading level. Students submit verbal or written reports on each book they read—and plot their progress on a wall chart.

For those who achieve their minimum monthly reading goal there is a certificate for a free "Personal Pan Pizza," good at any participating Pizza Hut restaurant. Other awards recognize students who achieve their minimum goal in three consecutive months. If an entire class achieves its goals in consecutive months, all students are invited to a free Pizza Hut pizza party.

"We're trying to encourage all children to read. We want to have a real and lasting, positive effect on the education of America's children," says Arthur G. Gunther, former chief executive officer of Pizza Hut.

His goal may be reached: More than five million students participated in the first year of the project.

Dupont. Science education is the concern of the Dupont Co., which recently turned its attention to science teachers. To help teachers keep current in their field, the company gave $50,000 to each school district near its major domestic operations so that teachers from those areas could attend one of their profession's most important gatherings, the annual meeting of the National Science Teachers Association.

Two federal programs for partners

Mutual school/business benefits are the goal of two federal programs.

The Job Training Partnership Act (JTPA) offers joint opportunities to schools and businesses for the operation of training programs for young people. Since the law requires that local councils be set up to match training with employment, it sets the stage for further joint projects.

Similar councils composed of business and education leaders are required under the Carl D. Perkins Vocational Education Act of 1984, a law that makes private industry a majority on the National Council on Vocational Education. The act also establishes technical committees, composed almost entirely of employers, to advise state boards of education on vocational education priorities and curriculum.

Partnerships

CBS. Spurred on by the parent company's interest in school partnerships, five CBS television stations recently signed up to adopt local schools and to generate more adoptions by broadcasting news about the partnerships to the entire community.

Exemplary of the effort was the adoption of Seward Park High School on the Lower East Side by New York's WCBS-TV. There, station workers first helped to redesign the school's television curriculum and then repaired broken and out-of-date video equipment. With that done, they taught how to use the fixed equipment on the new lessons—ultimately helping the students produce a documentary film.

The station also produced and broadcast public service announcements that featured chief executive officers of major New York corporations urging businesses to adopt schools. After the evening news, the station promoted the adopt-a-school concept in its editorials.

Dow Chemical Co. In one city where a Dow Chemical Co. plant is a major employer, secondary school science teachers can get field

---

Religious coalitions

If your school district is considering establishing a program of partnership between school and religious institutions, you may wish to consider these guidelines, developed at the Wingspread Conference on School/Church Partnerships (1985):

- Churches might encourage partnerships with the public schools provided they do not violate court rulings on the separation of church and state.
- These partnerships might be developed on an inclusive, interfaith basis or through a coalition to ensure that some religious groups do not dominate.
- Church/school partnerships should be based on a foundation of support for helping the community value children in society, since children are often overlooked, neglected, or abused, and treated primarily as consumers.
- Any partnership should be developed through open dialogue between the religious community and the public schools on how best to make a positive impact on the community. Common purposes and goals should be sought.
- Public schools should develop good guidelines for church/school partnerships that would prohibit proselytizing and any kind of religious indoctrination.
- Any help provided by outside resource persons should enhance the current curriculum of the schools and be under the direction of the teacher or other appropriate school personnel.
- Churches might provide volunteers to assist schools in dealing with significant issues; and promoting a commitment

National momentum

experience every summer in Dow's industrial internship program, a program that gives the company the benefit of the teachers' expertise as well. Near another plant site, retired Dow employees have signed up as school resource people in Dow's Education-Serve program.

Similar school partnerships are thriving in 20 communities where Dow plants are located, all at the prompting of Dow's chairman of the board, Robert Lundeen, whose longstanding interest in public education also led to the creation of the company's traveling display on "The Wonderful World of Chemistry."

Burger King Corp. The mutual benefits of school/business partnerships are alive and well with Jeffrey Campbell who, as chairman and chief executive officer of Burger King Corp., has launched projects that support top principals, teachers, and students.

Working with the National Association of Secondary School Principals, Burger King conducts an annual symposium for outstanding teachers and principals. Honorees at "In Honor of Excellence" are feted

---

to life-long learning, the value of teaching as a vocation, and the importance of a sound system of public education.
- Churches might wish to provide assistance for parents in understanding educational issues and how the public educational system serves as a foundation for a free and democratic society.
- Institutions that prepare the clergy and public school leaders should ensure that graduates understand the importance of the separation of church and state and are prepared to maintain it.
- Language should be developed making it clear that the integrity and independence of the public schools must be maintained, and that church groups should not attempt to dominate the public schools for religious purposes.
- A discussion of ways that schools and churches currently work in partnership might serve as a basis for further discussions.
- School leaders may wish to meet periodically with religious leaders in the community to provide information, answer questions, obtain advice, and seek cooperation on appropriate issues or concerns.

From Religion In The Public Schools, *a publication of the American Association of School Administrators, 1986.*

Partnerships

at Florida's posh Captiva Island resort.

For students, there's the company's "The Bonus That Lasts a Lifetime" program, which offers those who work on a Burger King restaurant crew an opportunity to get post-high school education at any accredited institution. To be eligible, crew members must complete six months of continuous service, averaging at last 15 hours of work a week, and, if in school, they must maintain at least a "C" average. The amount of money each employee can receive varies with length of service, but can amount to as much as $2,000.

High-achieving students and those with financial need are eligible for an additional scholarship that also can contribute up to $2,000 to their post-high school studies.

Burger King also funds a project for innovative programs in elementary and secondary schools, colleges, and universities. One such project, in Washington, D.C., high schools, resulted in a curriculum guide about "employability skills," which is now in use in a number of other districts.

National councils: Anyone interested in the job orientation of schooling has a national partner. . . .

With the advent of national corporate interests in local schools, the enduring interest of local citizens in their own schools has not diminished, but more often than not, these efforts are tied into national groups and programs.

Thousands of local citizens, representing business, unions, and government, work with a variety of councils, committees, and programs which aim at helping students ease into work.

"Next to the adopt-a-school program, joint school/business programs to help youth move from school to jobs comprise the largest number of partnerships," says Paul Barton, president of the National Institute for Work and Learning in Washington, D.C. "These programs, with all of their antecedent activities, have helped to keep education on young peoples' agendas until they are ready to work."

Such collaborative councils have appeared relatively recently, says Barton, who conducted a study on the subject for the National Commission for Employment Policy. He found that one major pilot project, which created and funded a number of community education/work councils from 1976 to 1979, stimulated the growth of numerous others. Most of these still exist. Still others grew out of efforts of the National Association for Industry-Education Cooperation.

Altogether more than 150 councils are active, training teachers to help students explore careers, providing career day resource people, setting up job placement services, and so on.

More than 30 councils are linked together in the Industry Education Council of California network, an intermediary between local and national programs that promote school/business partnerships. While local councils help students get ready for the job market and involve business leaders in school improvement, the intermediate-level council acts as a clearinghouse of local program information and national resources.

National momentum

Local councils are the pivotal group in another national effort founded by Thom McAn. Now 17 years old, the company's 70001, Ltd., project aims at getting schooling and jobs for school dropouts and young people on public welfare. More than 1,000 volunteers work with councils at nearly 60 sites. Enrollees attend regional and national training institutes where local business people work with them on employment interview skills, human relations, decision making, and oral communications. The national institutes have received government funding, but local funds support on-going activities at the 60 program sites.

Another national catalyst for local school/business collaboration is Public/Private Ventures, a Philadelphia, Pennsylvania-based group that uses mostly private and foundation funds to help nonproductive youth become self-sufficient. Youth from ages 14 to 15 were the first to participate in Ventures' pilot project, Summer Training and Education Program. Called STEP for short, the program offers two summers of academic remediation and instruction in life planning skills, plus work experience. The project, which exceeded expectations in its first year of operation and expanded dramatically the next, is based on this assumption: that negative academic experiences and adolescent parenthood lock in the target population to a life on nonproductivity . . . unless outside help is offered.

In the next chapter, such assistance—coordinated at the state level—promises even more partners for the schools.

Chapter 2

State leadership

The involvement of the business community with education at the state level has proliferated in recent years to include nearly every state in the union. The mutual effort has been serendipitous, indeed, lending clout to educational legislative initiatives and providing for local districts both models to emulate and programs to tap.
Consider:

- A group of corporate CEOs and leading educators, brought together through the *California Roundtable,* put their weight behind a major education reform package in that state and helped acquire more than $900 million in new money to fund it.
- The *Colorado Employability Skills Project,* a cooperative effort of the state department of education and the business community, is helping to pinpoint the skills businesses say they need in high school graduates and then working to ensure students have those skills.
- *Indiana Partners in Education,* launched by Gov. Robert Orr in 1984, offers training and consultation to communities that desire to establish partnership programs.
- Businesses in New York State that reach out to help teachers renew their skills during the summer have a partner themselves—the state government. Created by the legislature, the *Teacher Summer Business Training and Employment Program* reimburses 30 percent of the wages and associated benefits, up to $1,000 per teacher, to businesses or industries that hire teachers.

"More and more, education and business seem to be saying, 'We need each other,'" says Dow Chemical Co. Chairman Robert Lundeen, former co-chair of the Task Force on Education for Economic Growth and now head of the Michigan Partnerships for Education Task Force, a 13-member group of business, union, and education leaders.

And all states should have such task forces, Lundeen avers.

"The United States has difficult structural/economic problems with closely related social/educational problems that just won't go away by themselves," he comments. "We have aging industrial plants..., a decreasing tax base..., and unemployed workers."

These are serious problems, Lundeen continues, that can only be solved with innovation and effort. Cooperation between business and education, he feels, is one lever to pull to make it all happen.

In fact, it is happening in many states, and the following success stories tell how.

Partnerships

California: Business goes to bat for needed school funding. . . .

Could the recent major overhaul of the California public schools have occurred without the support of business, especially the *California Roundtable?*

Definitely not, declares state Supt. Bill Honig. Several years before the reform legislation became an issue, the business community "began to wake up to the fact that schools were being neglected by the broader interest in society" and realized they were going to be hurt by the backlash from that, he points out. But when the reform bill was put together, few thought business leaders would really go to bat for more money for school; even the Roundtable was split on the issue.

It was individual leaders within the Roundtable who really put their muscle and influence to work, Honig points out, eventually breaking a log jam on funding.

It all got started in 1979 when nearly 90 CEOs of major businesses in the state, organized through the Roundtable, appointed a Jobs and Education Task Force to study what needed to be done to improve California's public schools. Two years later, in the wake of a management study confirming that too many students in the state's high schools were not being adequately prepared for college or work, A.W. Clausen, president of BankAmerica, sat down with other leading corporate executives and inspired them to make a commitment unprecedented in the state's history.

The lobbying and other behind-the-scenes efforts to get additional state funding for education were the response of Roundtable members to the report on the aforementioned study of the status of high school graduates. The report had been adopted by the Roundtable board, setting into motion action on its four thrusts:

- Raising educational standards
- Upgrading technical education
- Increasing community involvement
- Reforming finance and strengthening the teaching profession.

Stephen Chaudet, director of public affairs for the Lockheed Corp., explained the commitment this way to a state school partnership forum: It has taken two decades for California's public education to deteriorate. . . . And it will take another decade for excellence and pride to be restored to our administrators, teachers, students, and communities regarding the educational process. Because this issue is so critical to our whole future as a state, the *California Roundtable* realizes it has to make this commitment for the long term.

New Jersey: Prestigious names lend a sense of mission. . . .

One of the most farsighted state efforts at developing partnerships is the *Public Responsibility for Educational Success* (PRES) project of New Jersey Gov. Thomas Kean's Leadership Commission. Indeed, the prestigious names on the commission—from Ernest Boyer, president of the Carnegie Foundation for the Advancement of Teaching; Gregory Anrig,

State leadership

president of the Educational Testing Service; and Edward Meade Jr. of the Ford Foundation, to Rutgers University President Edward Bloustein and Merck & Co. President John Huck—seem almost enough to guarantee success.

But the 50 commission members, whether they be presidents of higher educational institutions or state legislative leaders, are dedicated to hard work, not just letterhead clout, at improving higher education, the legal system, business, volunteers, the media, labor, families, social service institutions, and local government. This, truly, is partnering at its zenith.

"Our mission," said Huck at an organizational conference that drew more than 450 people from across the state, "is two-fold: first to develop a wide range of specific actions which our respective sectors of society can undertake to support the educational process, and, second, to see that some permanent mechanism exists to ensure this supportive interaction will continue into the future."

At present, the project is working at three levels:
- Providing information helpful to schools and nonschool institutions as they develop ways of working together
- Organizing networks of state, regional, and local groups interested in supporting education
- Identifying public policies that need to be considered by the governor and state legislature.

To get the word out and the project working, Rutgers University faculty have prepared background papers for the commission, while regional conferences have involved broad groups of people in its efforts. A newsletter on the project is being distributed to more than 50,000 educators, administrators, and community leaders. In addition, a handbook will describe partnership programs and contacts, while commission members and paid staff actually meet with school and nonschool organizations to initiate partnerships.

Wisconsin: A highly skilled work force is Parker Pen's goal. . . .

The commitment of one Wisconsin company teamed with strong leadership from the state department of education is behind a four-year effort to create "the finest, most skilled work force in America."

It is a lofty goal, indeed, but one that may bear fruition thanks to George Parker, president of the Parker Pen Company, and Herbert Grover, state school superintendent. It was in 1981 that Parker announced the *Parker Project,* an investment in time and money geared to making secondary and vocational education more relevant for students who soon would be entering the world of work. (More than 60 percent of Wisconsin's young people enter full-time employment soon after—or even before—completing high school. Ninety percent of them live and work within 25 miles of where they attended school.)

Funded with a $100,000 grant from Parker, matched by an equal amount from the state department of education, the project:
- Reviewed the research and available literature on the transition from school to work
- Surveyed 800 employers in the state about their experiences

Partnerships

with the employability of Wisconsin's youth
- Analyzed discrepancies between the preparation of students and the needs of employers
- Developed a series of recommendations for schools.

Once all of that was accomplished, the planning and coordination of the educational program were established, as were business and education partnerships, and the means of financing them all. The latter included launching the Governor's Council on Business-Education Partnerships to create local, regional, and state support groups to ensure that the recommendations are carried out. Parker contributed an additional $90,000 for this phase.

The Parker Project "began as an investigation of how Wisconsin youth are prepared for the world of work" and expanded to become the umbrella for "a new focus on major vocational education initiatives in the department of public instruction," was the assessment made by one supportive group, the Wisconsin Association of Manufacturers and Commerce.

Ohio: With flair, partnerships get their own "year"....

Having experienced great success with its "Year of Educational Excellence for All," the Ohio Department of Education followed with a year dedicated to *"You and Ohio Schools—Partners Building Excellence."* It focused on uniting parents and schools, working with agencies and the community work force, using local resources, enhancing teacher/student partnerships, and developing administrative and teacher partnerships.

To keep everyone abreast of what was happening, monthly packets of newsletters in each of these areas were mailed to local coordinators for dissemination, and a film that documented how schools were setting standards of excellence was distributed. By the end of the 1984-85 school year, the state education department could count hundreds of examples of new or strengthened partnership efforts throughout the state.

The partnership emphasis was launched through regional meetings to which a representative from each school district was invited. More than 400 districts subsequently appointed an advisory committee to cooperate with the state department on building partnerships. According to state Supt. Franklin Walter, commenting at the conclusion of the year, the partnership theme not only brought numerous benefits to people in education, but it also benefited people outside the school structure. He noted:

> Parents have received a better insight into what their children are learning, and employers have been given an opportunity to see whether current curricula are preparing students adequately for job market demands.

Nor were senior citizens or others without a direct link to the schools left out. "School-sponsored service projects and outreach programs have made these people realize that they, too, have a stake in the educational process," Walter added.

Concluded Ohio Gov. Richard Celeste: Partnerships "are now paying off in increased economic development for our state and in educational

State leadership

excellence for our schools. They are the basis of our strength and the springboard to educational excellence to which we are committed."

New York: No one model, but help for all. . . .

The *New York State Board of Regents* believes school-community partnerships are so important that it was one of the first to develop broad policy directions for such cooperative ventures.

The regents based their directions on four underlying assumptions:
- Schools are an integral part of the community. They reflect the strengths and problems of the communities that they serve.
- To a great extent, children's attitudes toward school and their readiness to learn are determined by family and neighborhood. Successful learning requires a close partnership between home, school, and community.
- Schools are an important community resource. They are familiar and accessible to nearly all community members and are supported by the community's tax dollars. Schools can play an important role in enriching the life of the community by collaboratively working and mobilizing resources to meet the needs of all members of the community—from preschoolers to senior citizens.
- There is no one model for building school/business partnerships. Successful partnerships are based on the unique needs and resources of each community.

While the regents' policy statement emphasizes that partnerships cannot be mandated from the state level, the assumption is made that the regents and the state education department can play a critical role in bolstering such ventures.

Minnesota: Despite controversy, business initiatives now thrive. . . .

The chief executive officers of some 60 large businesses, dubbed the *Minnesota Business Partnership,* got involved in education when they funded a study of grades K through 12 to the tune of $250,000, examining student performance, school operations, and possible changes. While some of the group's recommendations were controversial, the involvement of the business leaders provided an umbrella under which a number of creative initiatives are now thriving. For example:
- An assistant commissioner in the Minnesota Department of Education was given major responsibility for facilitating partnerships and collaborative efforts for school districts and other public and private agencies.
- The Education and Cultural Affairs Subcabinet was created by Gov. Rudy Perpich. It includes representatives of the University of Minnesota, the state university system, the state community college system, the board of vocational/technical education, the Higher

Partnerships

ESAs: Dedicated to partnerships

By its very definition, an educational service agency (ESA) encourages partnerships, points out David Hill, grants manager for the Erie I Board of Cooperative Educational Services in Lancaster, New York. Consequently, many ESAs have accomplished a worthy track record in matching community resources with schools, bringing public and private sectors together to work on mutual goals, and serving as partners themselves in cooperative job training or economic development councils.

For instance, a survey of Pennsylvania's 29 intermediate units revealed that all of them had active partnership agreements or activities, such as:

- Coordination of a cable TV series on career information spotlighting senior staff from area industries.
- The formation of a partnership between the county vocational school and the private industry council for sharing staff and conducting joint programs.
- With the help of the local Chamber of Commerce, identification of more than 100 private sector resources that could be used to help science and math teachers.
- Annual seminars to bring together superintendents and business executives to discuss mutual problems; a regional labor market survey; and customized job training programs for local business and industry.

The survey of the Pennsylvania units, conducted as part of a state effort to develop school partnerships, revealed the unique ability of the ESAs to bring people together—individual leaders from the private and public sectors, higher education, teachers, and civic groups.

This "people connection" also describes a highly successful partnership arrangement in another state, forged by the Educational Cooperative Service Unit of the Metropolitan Twin Cities Area in Minneapolis. Known as the Mentor Connection, the project matches 100 gifted students from the seven counties in the area with university, business, and community professionals.

The 18-week course gives students a chance to learn beyond the limits of their high school curriculum and provides access to professional leadership role models and awareness of education and career options. It is time-consuming for the mentors as well as the students, but the coordination by the Metro ECSU and its Gifted Center—and funding by 3M—have contributed stability and long-term commitment to the program. Ultimately the future economy and leadership of Minnesota will profit from the motivation provided to gifted young people.

State leadership

Education Coordinating Board, the Minnesota State Arts Board, and the state department of education.
- Through a Commissioner's Forum, the state education commissioner involves superintendents of local districts in monthly meetings to discuss trends and policy issues. Another monthly forum is for members of professional associations.
- Local program administrators are trained under the adult basic/community education section of the Minnesota Department of Education to collaborate with business and industry in developing course offerings and classroom sites.
- The Minnesota High Technology Council, a coalition of 115 high tech businesses, was formed to support educational efforts to help all students function better in a technological society.

Despite all the help from state and national organizations, most partners are local ones, as we'll see in Chapter 3.

Chapter 3

Local initiatives

While state and national partnership ventures are worthy of note, it is at the local level that the real work often gets done. Here is where the relationships developed between neighbors, between the school on Main Street and the business down the block, forge the link that binds community and school needs with local resources.

Sometimes it happens one very small step at a time; sometimes in giant leaps. Urban areas seem to have a head start. Nearly every urban district can tell of unprecedented and creative partnerships that are developing in their communities. Yet, according to a U.S. Department of Education survey of school partnership activities in 1984, fewer than 20 percent of the responding school districts with enrollments of 1,000 or less have active partnerships, compared to more than 80 percent of the largest districts. On the other hand, rural schools that do have partnerships have more schools participating in such arrangements, on a percentage basis, than urban districts.

There are several reasons for this situation. The kinds of resources that urban and suburban school districts can call on in their communities generally are nonexistent in rural areas. Only rarely is there a large corporate resource; businesses tend to be small and skill-specific, not lending themselves to broader training offered in schools. Further, according to rural education and demographic experts, the growing tendency for rural workers to commute to jobs in metropolitan areas is stripping schools of the volunteers and support base needed to promote ties between schools and communities.

The survey data, the Department of Education researchers concluded, "suggest the need for extra efforts to encourage the smaller, more rural districts to use community resources and perhaps suggest the greater need for these districts to look to regional alliances and statewide efforts in organizing such partnership efforts."

Whether big or small, the districts that responded to the AASA survey for this report made it clear that the essential ingredients for substantive involvement of economic and power influences within a community are strong, consistent communications—and hard work. There are untapped partnership possibilities and resources out there too numerous to contemplate—business, volunteer, civic, and professional associations that bolster the quality of the schools and the community around them. Each situation has its own story to tell.

Partnerships

Boston, Massachusetts: Rich in tradition but plagued by controversy over desegregation, this northeastern city's schools needed a unique "Compact" with public leaders....

For a turbulent decade, the Boston City Schools underwent upheavals that plunged its schools into a cycle of decline that appeared irrevocable. A controversial desegregation plan, a declining and changing student enrollment, and constant turnover in leadership boded nothing but ill for the schools.

But this is the city where the ideal of a common school came to fruition. Horace Mann is a revered name here; Boston Latin, the oldest, continuously operated public high school in the nation, maintains enviable standards. With more than 30 higher education campuses in its vicinity, Boston is a mecca for scholarly pursuits. The public schools might have been in trouble, but they were ripe for a visionary change.

Through the urging of then superintendent Robert "Bud" Spillane, whose background, incidentally, was academia and government service, businesses in Boston began to reach out in the early '80s, forming the Tri-Lateral Council for Quality Education to match every public high school with at least one business. It was among the first formally organized programs to link an outside community resource with an individual school—a movement known as adopt-a-school that has spread coast-to-coast.

The impetus behind adopt-a-school in Boston was a clear recognition by schools and business that something had to be done to decrease the school dropout rate, improve academic achievement, and increase the percentage of graduates pursuing higher education and those placed in jobs. Other segments of the Boston community, such as higher education institutions, linked with the schools also, but it was the business community that initially sought to help high school students adapt to the increasing competitiveness of academia and work in the Boston area.

The Tri-Lateral Council focused on long-term projects and strategies; no one promised miracles. Its most important contribution was laying the foundation for a unique collaboration between the schools and the Boston community—the Boston Compact. The Boston Compact is, simply stated, an agreement to work together. Its parties include the schools, business, higher education, labor, and the city government. Here are the commitments that make it work:

- The schools promise to improve attendance rates, lower dropout rates, and increase math and reading scores.
- Business and higher education promise to place students in jobs or enroll them on the campuses.

Has it worked? In the first two years of the Compact, 1,000 graduating seniors were placed in full-time jobs, and about 3,000 sophomores and juniors received private sector summer jobs through an agreement known as Job Collaborative. Moreover, the city's Private Industry Council supports a career teacher/counselor in almost every high school to provide year-round counseling, development, and job placement services.

Local initiatives

Another Compact activity, the Higher Education Agreement, has as its goal to increase by 25 percent in five years the number of Boston graduates who seek higher education. To achieve this, a Higher Education Information Center has been created to provide counseling, organize systemwide staff development institutes, establish a financial aid program and scholarships, and strengthen college retention efforts.

Still another Compact initiative is an agreement between 26 Boston trade unions and the public schools.

"Why are we spending so much time working with outside groups?" asked Spillane. "Because our constituency is no longer only the parent group. Our constituency is everyone in this community."

By the spring of 1985, just two years into the Compact, the school system could report that it was the beneficiary of corporate contributions totaling about $5 million, two of them the largest such contributions ever made to a public school system. To celebrate its 200th anniversary, the Bank of Boston gave the schools an endowment of $1.5 million—the interest of $300,000 each year is used for innovative programs not normally covered in the school budget. A $1 million endowment from the John Hancock Mutual Life Insurance Company will provide $100,000 a year for intramural athletics and reading programs in the city's middle schools.

Other spectacular gifts include IBM's investment of $1.5 million in a single elementary school to make it a national model for the use of high technology in elementary education. Another $1 million gift from the New England Mutual Life Insurance Company will help needy students bridge the gap between available resources and college costs.

Overall, the many in-kind services, counseling, training, donations, tutoring, and support for student activities organized through the Tri-Lateral Council are estimated to be worth $1.5 to $2 million a year.

Memphis, Tennessee: A southern city experiencing "white flight" and a changing student population had become demoralized. . . .

When Willie Herenton came to Memphis, Tennessee, as superintendent in 1979, he faced many odds. Because of court-ordered busing and other factors, the city's public schools had lost 35,000 white students within five years. Student achievement had declined, and public perceptions of the schools too often were either negative or apathetic. What's more, the business community had remained generally aloof from the schools' problems.

Herenton took it upon himself to hold out the first hand and asked the business community for help. He persuaded some of the community's power brokers to serve on a school/business advisory committee. He went to the chief executive officers of the city's major corporations and asked them to "loan" him their top public relations executives—"not their representative, but the person you use," he told them. The largest civic association in the city—the Memphis Rotary Club—was inspired to adopt the public schools as its special project.

Partnerships

Five years later, Herenton could affirm that "the odds are in our favor." All 158 schools in the Memphis system have been adopted by a business, civic, church, or government organization. The senior public relations executives put together a plan for the schools that contributed to the return of 3,000 white students within three years and a "dramatically improved image" within the community. The Rotary Club focused on boosting student and teacher morale through an extensive awards program. Student achievement in reading and math has improved every year since the schools became a "cause" with community leaders.

The adopt-a-school program was particularly successful, according to Herenton, because it enabled a true cross-section of people to become acquainted with the schools. For example:

- The East Memphis Senior Center adopted kindergarten classes at nearby Norris Elementary School.
- The Colonial Baking Co., among several projects with the Klondike Elementary School, sponsored a field trip to the Huntsville Space Center for students who improved their grades.
- Baptist Memorial Hospital sponsored the first Student Health Fair at Manassas High School with hospital staff conducting a variety of health screening tests for the 800 students.
- First Tennessee provided summer intern jobs and helped with senior job interviews at Craigmont High School.
- To promote attendance and good behavior, the Memphis Welcome Wagon turned part of the Lincoln Junior High cafeteria into a restaurant as a special treat for students with high achievement. Welcome Wagon also helped compose and print a student handbook.

Under the direction of Barbara Russell, the adopt-a-school program added "friends"—those companies or organizations with services to offer all of the Memphis schools. Big Star Supermarkets, for example, established tours for students to help them understand the food industry. Other companies have donated surplus or discontinued equipment that is placed in a central warehouse and drawn on for use in adopt-a-school projects.

The Memphis program is a "people" program, not a money program, according to Russell. She and other program coordinators suggest these essential ingredients:

- A strong superintendent committed to community involvement
- A well-known business leader able to open corporate boardroom doors and willing to set up interviews with business leaders
- A program director dedicated to the program's purpose and who can articulate its needs to the business community
- Principals convinced that community involvement can be effective and will not interrupt the education process.

"The adopt-a-school program has created a family between the school system and the business, civic, religious, and military communities in Memphis," says Russell. "No longer can it be considered a backward, river city."

Local initiatives

Projects with pizzazz

It is hard to single out the best partnerships projects from among the more than 46,000 in operation across the country. But the following are certainly worthy of note:

- *The Learning Exchange in Kansas City, Missouri.* Begun in 1972 by two teachers in a church basement, this program has grown to a large facility with a professional staff of 35. Two-thirds of the $1 million annual budget comes from contracts with school districts and services to educators; the rest is provided by some 200 businesses, foundations, and individuals in the community. The scope of the exchange is broad—college credit courses, workshops for teachers and students, teacher consultations, assistance to school advisory committees, an Exchange City wherein 12,000 fifth graders each year operate the business for a day, and a computer consortium.
- *The Cleveland Scholarship Program, Inc.* Founded in 1954 and supported by local foundations and businesses, this metropolitan-wide program raised almost $600,000 in 1984 and is the country's largest private program to help students secure post-high school education. The program supports advisors in more than 30 area high schools who help students find the college funds they need. The program also supplements funding sources for students, but it doesn't stop there. At college, students being helped by the program are given continuing support and counseling and provided with summer jobs. After graduation, the program helps with job placement and references to prospective employers.
- *The Academic Internship Program in Charlotte-Mecklenburg, North Carolina.* Begun in 1975, this program now averages 400 placements for students in community hospitals, museums, government agencies, local business and industry, and schools. Students spend an average of six hours a week with their community sponsor.
- *Community leadership in South St. Paul, Minnesota.* This is a "beyond business and education" approach to community development whereby the schools are partners with city government, the chamber of commerce, the housing and development authority, retail businesses, and other groups and associations. One outcome has been Leadership South St. Paul, the first leadership development program to select emerging community leaders for a nine-month training program to increase their community awareness, understanding of leadership theory, and leadership skills.

Partnerships

Seattle, Washington: A richly diverse city finds a place and a way for everyone to help the schools. . . .

On a given day in March, the doors of the junior and senior high schools in Seattle, Washington, burst open as students eagerly depart for businesses throughout the city where they will spend time working and learning as part of the annual Mentorship Day. Every school in the district has a partner and, on Mentorship Day, companies host as many as 100 students from their partner school.

Seattle's conduit to partnering is the Private Initiatives in Public Education (PIPE), organized in 1980 by the Seattle Chamber of Commerce. PIPE's board of directors includes business partners; the school district; associations for principals, teachers, and PTAs; the Municipal League; the Seattle Urban League; and the chamber.

All sorts of activities are channeled through PIPE, and, as the partnerships develop, so do common themes—an awareness of the different worlds of each partner; the formation of a bonding process as the partners settle into the relationship; a concentration on projects that enhance class curriculum, career awareness, student motivation, and moral building; and the development of reciprocal offerings from the schools. For example:

- Peoples Bank provides monthly speakers to Ballard High School and advises parents on student loans.
- The advanced science class at Roosevelt High School receives background material on lab work and medical technology from the Children's Orthopedic Hospital.
- Pacific Northwest Bell arranges for American government classes at Cleveland High School to visit the Seattle municipal courts and city council.
- With the help of their Boeing Company partner, Ranie Beach High School and South Shore Middle School host a team of actors from the Oregon Shakespearean Festival.

As in Memphis and elsewhere, PIPE's program includes a partners-at-large program to channel resources from businesses, labor organizations, restaurants, art groups, social service agencies, and others unable to support an individual partnership project. These resources are handled through the resource skills bank.

PIPE, like other partnering groups, focuses on this sharing of resources rather than merely financial support for the schools. It has promoted and organized shadowing opportunities for students, in-depth interning experiences, special workshops for faculty and students at business sites, and guest speakers on personal and career topics.

Greater Wilmington, Delaware: Public confidence in schools was shaken by a desegregation fight but restored by a coordinated business/schools effort. . . .

The Greater Wilmington Development Council described itself as a "solution-finder." Founded in 1960, for more than 20 years it was a

Local initiatives

private, nonprofit public interest organization that identified and analyzed community problems, set priorities, and developed solutions and actions to deal with them. Its directors came from business and industry, professions, various institutions, and civic organizations.

For several years (the GWDC no longer exists), one of its priorities was public education. As in other cities adjusting to desegregation and a changing student population, public support for the schools had dwindled. In fact, after a metropolitan-wide desegregation plan took effect, a large voter turnout defeated a school tax referendum by a 10-1 margin. School enrollment in the affected districts decreased by more than 36 percent in five years, while private school enrollment jumped 22 percent.

In 1982 the Greater Wilmington Development Council swung into action. Working with the Wilmington and four surrounding school districts, the council adopted the Education Project, now an independent community effort. Its purpose was clearcut: to determine how the private sector could help the districts improve their services and to improve public perceptions of the schools.

Within two years the project had invested more than $300,000—from local and national foundations, the school districts themselves, the state, and companies within the council—for a variety of efforts. It sponsored three basic research projects—a study of community, teacher, and employer attitudes toward the schools; a study of the county's school resources; and a study of school/business partnerships in more than 50 cities—as well as a series of forums for educators and community/business leaders to discuss the findings and develop their own plans. These became the Education Project. To boost community confidence, the project:

- Targeted a series of newsletters on public education to 1,500 local decision makers
- Arranged a series of in-depth school tours for corporate executives and major realtors
- Prepared a thorough and sophisticated Cultural Resources Guide for teachers to encourage them to use community resources
- Developed business sponsorship of curriculum improvement in computer technology and mathematics
- Established a Principals' Center to improve the management skills of school administrators
- Used radio to reach the community—"drive-time" radio features on public education four times a week and a monthly one-hour talk show on a specific issue
- Initiated a mini-grant program for teachers to support innovative classroom projects
- Established a School Recognition Program to provide a small grant and public recognition to the eight schools with the greatest improvement in attendance, student retention, and achievement
- Helped develop a project to involve volunteers in tutoring.

A year after this project began, there were signs it was working. Public school enrollments were above predictions; private school enrollments

Partnerships

declined for the first time in eight years; new funding sources and media attention developed; and the attitudes of the involved organizations were positive.

After continuing for several years as an effort of the development council, The Education Project became a separate entity, and the districts involved agreed to jointly develop a Regional Learning Facility governed by an Education Partnership, with representatives from the participating school boards, the state department of education, and the development council.

Jackson, Mississippi: Partnerships grow from one to many. . . .

The Jackson, Mississippi, adopt-a-school program began with one high school and the Allstate Insurance Company back in 1978. Today, the district's many partnerships involve business, religious, and civic groups throughout the city. The benefits to the school district—and the community—are many, says Supt. Robert N. Fortenberry, and some of the most important benefits are intangible ones: "It is difficult to measure, but impossible not to see, the increased self-esteem a student or teacher can feel when someone 'out there' cares enough to get involved personally in the work of the school."

The district's adopt-a-school program includes many ideas for partnership activities that community service groups can undertake, such as landscaping of school grounds, gift-giving at nursing homes, spaghetti supper fundraisers, staff/employee ball games, purchase of shares of school newspaper stock, sponsorship of Christmas parade floats, and donations of artwork.

The Jackson program also outlines projects to demonstrate appreciation of the adopting company. These include featuring the adopting company and their employees in the school newspaper; giving luncheons and coffees; awarding honorary PTA memberships and offices; providing school gym privileges for employees; providing student entertainment (band, choir, etc.) for service projects; supplying company Christmas cards designed by students; and presenting Christmas stockings and other seasonal treats.

Greater Baltimore, Maryland: An inner-city school system finds that its business leaders want to learn from school leaders how to help students. . . .

In many ways, the Baltimore schools serve as a model of how well school/business partnerships can work across the entire spectrum of school activities. This is a serious, businesslike effort in a district that is a $340 million business itself. It includes an adopt-a-school program initiated by the Greater Baltimore Committee in the 1970s, twice-monthly luncheon meetings (the Dialogue Group) where 20 high-level business executives meet with the school superintendent and school board president, and various business task forces that provide management and technical help to the schools.

Local initiatives

Why is the business community willing to commit so much time and resources to the schools? George B. Hess Jr., president of Hess Shoes and chairman of the Dialogue Group, explains it this way: "We can no longer sit by and complain about poor education. For us to have the top flight school system that business needs requires the involvement of everyone."

That involvement encompasses more than 70 partnerships between schools and the business community. For example:

- Southern High School and the Baltimore Gas and Electric Co. The company teaches the basics of filling out job applications and other activities to ninth graders, prepares lesson plans to improve math and verbal skills, sends teams of employees to visit the schools a half-day each week, supplies guest speakers and hosts field tours, and provides part-time jobs to students with excellent attendance and academic records.
- Eutaw-Marshburn Elementary School and The Baltimore Life Insurance Co. The company staff prepared materials for each grade level to emphasize math and verbal skills. Students visit company headquarters, and company personnel frequently are at the school. Employees also attend regular PTA meetings and help keep parents informed about all activities.
- Federal Hill Elementary School and Coopers and Lybrand. Staff people from this accounting firm help students produce their own school newspaper, with students who excel in reading and language skills alternating as monthly editors. The firm prints the newspaper.
- Northeast Middle School and WBAL-TV. The station donates surplus equipment to the school and has built a production set for a school news station, helping students develop skills in all phases of television production. WBAL's on-air personalities appear regularly on the school's morning broadcast; students at "NEMS-TV" have received awards in city and state film festivals.

Task forces also have been an important part of the Greater Baltimore Committee's efforts. A School Image Task Force, for example, recommended a communications plan for the school district. Elsewhere, a task force that analyzed the school district's personnel office, at the request of the superintendent, resulted in revisions and modernization as well as a program to honor three outstanding principals with cash and public recognition.

Probably the most significant and long-lasting contribution was the committee's task force on state aid. The committee entered an *amicus curiae* brief on behalf of the Baltimore school district in a state education funding equity case; testified before the state legislature for additional aid for the school district; and pledged to continue this kind of support.

Another major item on the committee's agenda is its attention to citywide vocational education programs, particularly the planning, construction, and curriculum of the Westside Skill Center. The committee also stands ready to conduct research on compelling school district issues, having assigned a task force to look at the delegation of authority to principals and their selection process. Another group advised the

Partnerships

school district on its data processing administration, and yet another made recommendations on school purchasing procedures.

Salem, Oregon: Even a smaller community can put together partnerships . . . without the status of a Fortune 500 company. . . .

What about those cities and communities without a Fortune 500 company and the vast resources in personnel, money, prestige, and political leverage such partnerships bring?

No matter, said William Kendrick, then superintendent of Salem, Oregon, School District 24J. Small businesses are just as willing and helpful, he found out, and a list of Salem school partners bears this out: Anderson's Sporting Goods, Ashton Photo, Bob's Hamburgers, Madrona Dental Building, Salem Pediatric Clinic, Stayton Canning, Sunshine Pizza, Boone Road Nursery, Willamette University, Oregon Department of Commerce, and the *Statesman-Journal.*

Kendrick appointed a task force of 15 business people and, with the help of the Salem Area Chamber of Commerce, established a Business Partnership Program to accompany the school district's well-organized volunteer and community education programs.

"This is a high-touch program," says Kendrick, "dependent more on contacts among people than on money for the schools."

Through closer contact with schools, business people gain a greater appreciation of the schools while students gain positive views of the free enterprise system, Kendrick believes. "The partnership is good for the economy, education, and business. It makes sense to join hands in an effort where everyone comes out a winner."

Nashville, Tennessee: A school district in trouble reaches out quickly to learn how to use partnerships. . . .

When the Metropolitan Nashville-Davidson County public schools faced unprecedented change—a totally new board, taking office amidst enactment of a desegregation plan, school closings, and budget slashes—plans were made immediately to involve the entire Nashville community in supporting the schools.

Civic and educational leaders formed a committee that began collecting information on partnerships around the country while volunteers attended workshops on partnership organization. Meanwhile, a nonprofit organization to enroll the private sector in support of the schools was formed. Dubbed PENCIL, for Public Education Nashville Citizens Involved in Leadership, it had four objectives:
- Establish an adopt-a-school program in the Metro area (by 1985, all schools had been "adopted")
- Introduce the public to school board candidates
- Publicize positive programs taking place in Metro schools
- Support efforts to implement the desegregation plan.

Once these initial goals had been reached, PENCIL focused its attention on other projects, such as a teacher awards program, funded by the Hospital Corporation of America, and a special partnership with local

Local initiatives

military organizations to help young, unemployed students gain technological skills as well as attitude skills. PENCIL counselors spend an hour each day with enrollees and help place them in jobs after training.

PENCIL also supports a program called Jobs for Tennessee Graduates. Patterned after a project that began in Delaware, this program enrolls non college-bound students who have a desire to learn but who are likely to have difficulty finding jobs. The high school seniors spend a minimum of three hours a week with a PENCIL jobs specialist who provides career counseling, helps develop a student's employability skills, and acts as a motivator. Students in the program have their own career associations, and a computerized job bank helps fit students to job openings.

District of Columbia: Hands on with the business community, not a handout. . . .

Adopted by an embassy. . . by the U.S. Department of Education. . . by the National Science Foundation. . . by the Department of Defense. . . by the President of the United States.

There is one school district in the country where such remarkable linkages could occur. But these headline-getters are only a small part of the broad community involvement painted by Supt. Floretta McKenzie of the District of Columbia schools. There are more than 40 federal agency school adoptions in place, but the exemplary part of the District of Columbia program is the corporate involvement.

"In our approach to the corporate world, we started with the common sense proposition that people form partnerships to reduce costs and to reap mutual gains, not to subsidize one another," McKenzie explains. "We knew, therefore, what we didn't want from the business community. We didn't want a handout."

In fact, McKenzie believes that it is the schools' expectations of charity that gives school/business relationships a maligned image. "Often the partnership in truth is philanthropy, volunteerism, or mere window-dressing," she comments. "Corporate involvement must not be a one-way street with schools on the receiving end of corporate benevolence. That kind of partnership is doomed to failure. Productive relationships seldom endure without a quid pro quo."

That is why financial contributions rank way down on the list of how private sector partners can participate in the District's programs, says McKenzie. More important to the schools is the help businesses provide with curriculum design, liaison with other businesses in the same field, paid employment opportunities for students and new graduates, technical support, and classroom instruction.

The District's private sector involvement focuses on its high school career program. These school-within-a-school programs at five high schools stress basic skills, refinement of the curriculum to address potential employers' needs, employability training, and rigorous academic preparation. Each program has a lead business sponsor, backed by as many as 60 other companies or organizations; the total investment

Partnerships

from the private sector over a four-year period has been more than $3 million.

Each career program's advisory board of industry leaders is actively involved in curriculum development, staff training, and program design and management. The boards also provide internships for students and "externships" for teachers. The career programs include:

- Business/finance at Woodson High School, emphasizing accounting, banking, bookkeeping, insurance, and market analysis. Partners: Blue Cross/Blue Shield and the D.C. Bankers Association.
- Communications at McKinley/Penn School, emphasizing advertising, broadcast journalism, broadcast engineering, photography, and print journalism. Partners: C & P Telephone, community foundations, Goldberg/Marchesano Associates, National Home Library Association, WJLA, the Xerox Corporation, and Time, Inc.
- Health professions at Eastern High School, emphasizing dentistry, medical business professions, medical technology, medicine, nursing, nutrition, physical therapy, and public health service. Partners: Capitol Hill Hospital, D.C. General Hospital, George Washington University College of Medicine and Medical Center, and the Howard University College of Allied Health Sciences.
- Hotel management/culinary arts at Roosevelt High School. Partners: Culinary Institute of America, Hotel Association of Washington, D.C., and the Private Industry Council.
- Pre-engineering at Dunbar High School, including chemical, civil, electrical, and industrial engineering. Partners: Alfred Sloan Foundation, Dunbar Alumni Association, General Motors, Goddard Space Center, Howard University, IBM, METCON, PEPCO, and the University of the District of Columbia.

The District's Public/Private Partnership Program also has the backing of major corporations, associations, and foundations for staff development and leadership training. They support a Management and Staff Development Institute and provide training for teachers in private industry as well as loan personnel for special training projects. Another initiative is in the area of educational technology, with corporations helping to increase the computer literacy of administrators, teachers, and students. Corporations also underwrite arts presentations in the schools as well as instructional workshops and artist-in-residence programs.

Noting that businesses in the United States are estimated to spend $60 million a year on training programs, some of it remedial, McKenzie declares:

> "In the D.C. public schools we argue that corporations ought to replace their remedial education costs with investments in basic education. By supporting improvements in the schools, corporations can expect to profit from an improved labor force, lower training costs, reduced turnover rates, and more productive employees."

Local initiatives

Chicago, Illinois: Self-worth for a troubled school from Sara Lee. . . .

Dallas. Houston. Chicago. Oakland. Memphis. Adopt-a-school programs seem almost synonymous with the names of some of the largest school districts in the country where the leadership of the superintendent, a willing business community, and commitment of professional staff from both school and business sectors ensure success.

How an adoption matures from token efforts to a full-blown partnership—with the support of well-organized programs at the citywide level—is illustrated by Chicago's Harper High School.

This was a school near the bottom in achievement, suffering "years of despair," according to a *Chicago Tribune* account. The dropout rate exceeded 50 percent, more than a third of the students were failing two or more courses a year, and the principal estimates that one of four female students would become pregnant during the school year.

Yet its percentile rank on reading scores moved up nine points recently, the first glimmer that the hope being pumped into the school by its business partner—the Sara Lee Corporation—might be working.

The partnership with Sara Lee had a typical beginning. The company had just decided to participate in the adopt-a-school program when approached by Principal Donald Mulvihall whose optimism wasn't high. "I knew once they heard about our problems, they would want to adopt some other school," he recalls, "but our students, parents, and teachers gave them such a sad story, they went nowhere else."

It began with a company employee speaking monthly to the school's business education class. But the company was seeking a way to reach all of the 1,300 students and decided to fund two $6,000 scholarships for students, grants for teachers to use in the classroom, and scholarships for teachers to improve their skills. By 1985, the company was providing $32,000 in support to the school. Moreover, Sara Lee launched a project whereby students formed "corporations" and invented new projects. The winning corporation was awarded a share of Sara Lee stock.

The company next conceived the Academic Team to reward students who achieve academically and encourage others to do so. Chicago Bears wide receiver Willie Gault (who was earning $1.3 million in his pro job) served as captain of the team, visiting the school to meet with students, helping them write a team song and cheer, and distributing "I Got Smart" sweatshirts—all for a $1,000 retainer.

Rural America: They may not be called partnerships, but in rural America close ties with the community never went out of style. . . .

The Amboy-Good Thunder High School's journalism class regularly prepares two pages for the weekly *Country Times* in Blue Earth, Minnesota. They write the articles, lay out the pages, and, if time permits, sell and design the ads. According to the *Country Times* editor, this arrangement creates excellent public relations for the school—and the school news pages are the first read section of the paper.

Partnerships

This is typical of many partnership activities that exist throughout the country in rural areas. They're often small in scope, very personal and intimately tied to the community. In people resources, rural schools are richly endowed.

Moreover, there may be more such relationships than popularly believed. The first Partnerships in Education forum sponsored by the President's Advisory Council on Private Sector Initiatives focused on partnerships for quality education in rural America. Among the showcase projects:

- *Texas Tech Co-op for More Effective Schools.* Texas Tech University and Pedamorphosis, Inc., a nonprofit corporation that promotes school improvement, is working with eight rural Texas Panhandle school districts to provide effective school leadership and training for administrators and teachers.
- *Teacher-Professor Class Exchange.* East Carolina University and seven public school systems in rural northeast North Carolina have an exchange program whereby university faculty rotate teaching assignments in the public schools; public school teachers, in turn, share their expertise on campus.
- *Dixie College/Garfield School District Tele-Learning Project.* An example of how rural schools are adopting technology as a solution to their isolation, this project links the Garfield School District in Panguitch, Utah, to Dixie College and the Utah State Office of Education. Using dedicated data and conference lines, college faculty are instructing students in tele-learning centers at their isolated school sites in subjects not normally available at the schools. The initial project provided trigonometry instruction at Garfield and two other high schools.
- *Kickapoo Technical Assistance Program.* The partners are the Center for Public Affairs at the University of Kansas and the Kickapoo tribe in Kansas with the purpose of providing educational program planning for the tribe and the Kickapoo Nation School, as well as help on curriculum development.

Rural Iowa: Showcasing a few of the 16 partnerships that are thriving in the Iowa countryside....

In April 1985, Iowa Gov. Terry Branstad and the Iowa Department of Public Instruction presented a showcase of partnerships for more than 400 education and community leaders. Among the programs cited:

- *Amana School/Business/Community Partnership.* The school district here functions as a human resource agency serving all citizens, regardless of age, "who wish to grow and improve." Programs include meals for the elderly, a preschool daycare, a school/community library, and several community education and recreation activities. The district loans equipment and meeting room space and provides student help for entertainment, art services, and special events. It also offers grant-writing and consultant services for the community.

Local initiatives

- *CAL Theater and Concert Series.* The CAL Community School District, at Latimer, concentrating on cultural enhancement for the community, works with the local chapter of People United for Rural Education and the Iowa Arts Council to bring performing artists to the community. The school district provides facilities, administration, clerical, and maintenance support services. PURE provides volunteers for planning and organization. The arts council supplements the series so performances can be affordable even to small audiences. The community provides meals, housing, and related costs for the performing artists.
- *Project Home Town Study.* A partnership of the Kirkwood Community College, Bennett Community School District, and Bennett community civic organizations provides college credit courses, associate of arts degree programs, advanced high school classes, adult and community education programs, and continuing education classes for everyone in the Bennett community. The programs are beamed via microwave TV from one or more colleges and schools in Iowa. In 1985, there were 16 schools involved, allowing much greater flexibility in the curriculum.

Turning the "adoption" tables

Adoptions between schools and community organizations often put students in an adoptive role—and the benefits can be far reaching.

Take, for example, the partnership between Abraxas, California, High School and the Rancho Bernardo Convalescent Hospital. Within five months of the start of the program, director Steven Levy reported that attendance at this continuation high school was up appreciably, as much as 40 percent.

Because more than 80 percent of the students come from broken homes, the opportunity to give to others has been a positive influence on their attitudes, Levy reported. In fact, students became so involved that they were giving up evenings and weekends to work on the project and initiated many new programs for the elderly at the home. The project is so popular that a waiting list of students who wanted to work there developed in short order and a group has formed to meet at the high school twice a week to discuss the elderly and aging.

Student pride in their school, which had image problems of its own, was given a boost as well, Levy reported.

Partnerships

West Point, Virginia: A small town finds a unique way to boost science, math training. . . .

The Virginia State Department of Education, concerned about the growing shortage of science and math teachers, was seeking a site for a model corporate partnership project to bolster math and science teaching. It chose the rural West Point schools, a district of just 750 students in two schools. The town itself, with a population of 2,500, is dependent economically on the Chesapeake Corporation whose corporate offices and major pulp and paper mill are located there.

The already established economic connection between the corporation and the schools added another link when the two partners agreed on a half-day teaching plan. Initiated in 1983, this meant that Chesapeake provides a company employee, who has computer science training, to teach up to three hours a day in the West Point schools. The schools set the curriculum needs; the Chesapeake teacher participates in whatever inservice training is required. (For its part, the state department of education offers guidance and provides flexibility in regulations to allow noncertified teachers to participate.)

In exchange for the borrowed teacher, the school provides facilities and personnel for inservice training of Chesapeake employees, organizes a physical fitness program for employees, and offers school grounds, facilities, and equipment use to the corporation upon request.

Suburbia: Neither city nor rural, don't think these districts are left out of the action. . . .

Are suburban districts squeezed out of partnership action because of their location on the edges of towns and cities? The answer is no as the Montgomery County, Maryland, schools prove. A suburb of Washington, D.C., Montgomery County has developed an extensive mentor/internship program for gifted students that places them throughout the metropolitan area.

Elsewhere, the West Suburban Business-Education Partnership, encompassing three suburban school districts in the Minneapolis area and the West Suburban Chamber of Commerce, shows that not all the action is downtown. This partnership emphasizes equal exchange of resources and began with a survey by the chamber of the educational resources of businesses in the area, as well as school facilities that businesses might like to use.

Based on the survey, the partnership got underway with an internship program and "shadowing" program for students and a training program for businesses. The project hired a part-time coordinator, and the activities grew to include help on curriculum development, guest speakers and instructors, company tours, time off for parents to be involved in school activities during school hours, and use of company equipment and facilities.

In turn, the schools have offered businesses conference and recreation facilities, child care programs, computer access and training, career

Local initiatives

centers, staff training, audiovisual and cable TV facilities, and special interest seminars.

As the sharing increases, so do the ideas for partnership activities, says Betty Bothereau, director of community education in the St. Louis Park, Minnesota, schools (known throughout the country for its partnership arrangement with the giant Honeywell Corporation). Other schools participating in the West Suburban project are the Hopkins and Minnetonka districts.

Chapter 4

Additional partners

School partnerships assume many different disguises. As we have already seen, they are not limited to simple sharing or philanthropy arrangements between local businesses and the schools. They encompass every sector of the community—from government to private enterprise to nonprofit institutions. Nor are they always called "partnerships." They may be referred to as consortiums, alliances, forums, roundtables, ventures, associations, or initiatives. But whatever the terminology, they all basically mean the same thing: joining forces to share resources in mutually beneficial ways.

The simplest and most straightforward are the local partnerships handled on a community or district basis. In Chapter 3, we examined a number of these. We've also taken a look at partnerships organized at the state level, usually involving the state education agency in some fashion, and those with a more national perspective.

But there are others that merit examination as well; partnerships involving higher education, foundations, and individual volunteers that take the concept of partnering beyond the stereotypical school/business model (an eminently successful one, to be sure) to encompass the entire community.

Foundations: Uncovering new sources of financial support. . . .

Wake County, North Carolina, school Supt. Robert Bridges, faced an interesting dilemma. An alumnus of one of the oldest high schools in Raleigh, now a Wall Street executive, had presented his alma mater with $100,000—and almost no strings attached.

The problem was how to accept a monetary gift of that size. Bridges did accept—and then turned to the Wake County Education Foundation to administer an endowment program for the school that included two teaching "chairs" with annual bonuses of $5,000 from the endowment's interest. The Wake County Education Foundation, formed in 1983, was created to receive and raise money from the private sector for the schools. With $350,000 in assets, it funds mini-grants for teachers, teacher recognition awards, math excellence awards, and a $1,000 scholarship to a graduating senior at each high school.

The Wake County Foundation is an example of the growing number of homegrown foundations established on behalf of the public schools. Some believe the idea took root in Beverly Hills, California, following cutbacks resulting from the passage of Proposition 13, but there had

Partnerships

been some traditional foundation approaches to raising money in local school districts long before that.

By 1984, according to a survey by the Foundation Center, nearly 2,000 foundation grants of $5,000 or more had been made by 301 foundations to public and private schools, agencies, associations, and other pre-college educational institutions.

California led the states in foundation support, receiving 331 grants totaling $10.7 million. Two-thirds of the grants were for program development; one-third for capital support. The Boston-Washington corridor is another hospitable place for foundation giving: 62 percent of all foundations are located there.

Partnership Projects. One national project funded by foundations represents a partnership among the foundations themselves. Known as Partnership Projects, these are 19 local programs that bring resources together to prevent youth unemployment. Locally designed and administered, the programs nonetheless share these characteristics:

- Business takes the lead in raising money, creating jobs, and training staff.
- Schools refer students, provide classroom space, and sometimes pay teachers and give academic credit.
- Foundations provide seed money, evaluation, training, and travel.
- Small amounts of foundation money often lead to larger amounts of local and federal aid.

Allegheny Conference. Since 1978, Pittsburgh, Pennsylvania, has experienced enormous success from its education foundation program, the Allegheny Conference Education Fund. Through this program, the Pittsburgh corporate community rallied support for the schools with several initiatives: public information about the schools, mini-grants to teachers, school/business adoptions, discretionary funding for innovative schools and school projects, and an educator-in-residence series that brought well-known educators to the community for discussions of critical issues facing the schools.

The Allegheny Education Fund ultimately led to more ambitious things. If a well-conceived local foundation dedicated to community involvement with the public schools worked so well in Pittsburgh, why not elsewhere? David Bergholz, who helped spearhead creation of the Education Fund, answered that by persuading other foundations to create the Public Education Fund, a five-year experiment that provides seed money and technical assistance to encourage the development of local education funds across the country, but particularly in urban areas.

"It is a smart money approach," says Bergholz. Initially, he notes, local foundations were used by schools to make up for lost funds (such as in California). Now they are seen as a way for community forces to make a contribution to local school improvement. Nonetheless, he warns, the purposes of too many new foundations are not well thought out: "All the energies go into writing bylaws for Sec. 504c."

Additional partners

Also, Berholz feels, foundations need to establish their independence from the school system early, remaining both "friendly and neutral" toward the system. The foundation must create trust with the outside community because it may find itself serving as the intermediary or broker between "irate taxpayers and irate parents."

Another offshoot of Pittsburgh's experience with the Education Fund was the adoption of that model for an entire state. The West Virginia Education Fund, established in 1983, was the first in the country to attempt to marshal foundation resources statewide. Arizona quickly followed suit, and Kentucky and Alabama now have active foundation efforts.

West Virginia's effort. In West Virginia, the corporate community readily bought into the concept. The president of the board of directors is an executive with the Union Carbide Corporation, and board members represent coal, steel, power, government, and education interests. The initial funding goal was $190,000, and half that had been raised within one year of operation (initial funding came primarily from the Benedum Foundation, Ashland Oil and Ford foundations, and the New York Community Trust).

And finally, schools still uncertain about the role of foundation support can take courage from Sandra Hartley, president of the Paola, Kansas, school board, as she explained why this small community had established an Endowment Association: "We believe the public must continue to be financially responsible for the fundamentals of their system of public education. . . . The role of the Endowment Association is to enhance the quality of education, not to replace public funding."

Volunteers: Today, as always, people resources have been essential for schools. . . .

Gaithersburg, Maryland. It bothered Ralph Nash, a physicist with the National Aeronautics and Space Administration, that the young people in his neighborhood had little interest in science. They told him it was dull; he decided that the real problem was uninspired teaching.

So Nash decided to take action and opened his home in Gaithersburg, Maryland, every Saturday to help students—first the original eight youngsters, then more—explore the "fun side of science."

Nash began his program in his kitchen in 1973. The project expanded to become Adventures in Science, a nonprofit organization now serving more than 100 students at four locations. When the program became too big for his house, Nash, now retired, enlisted the aid of the Commerce Department's National Bureau of Standards, located some five minutes from his home. The bureau offered the use of classrooms and laboratories; other area businesses have followed suit.

Nash's long list of volunteers—from computer scientists and chemists to physicists and dentists—help the children, ages 9 to 15, share the ideas they learned in school and expand on them in an exploratory way. At the annual Parents Day that culminates a year's work, the Saturday

Partnerships

students have presented projects in weather predicting, cheese making, how the eye works, holograms, electronics, and robotics. Moreover, Nash has prepared a start-up package to help interested volunteers establish these types of programs elsewhere.

Whatever the partnership, people have always been the catalyst, the essential ingredient for getting things done. The public school system evolved from just such individual and community commitment to education for all. But structures for channeling involvement with the schools have changed—from informal to formal, from almost exclusively parents (and predominantly mothers) to nonparent interests, from token efforts to substantive involvement and funding.

The growth and maturity in the relationships between schools and volunteers resulted to a large extent from the experience and knowledge base accumulated by individuals and associations over the years. Substantial resources are now available from such groups as the National Community Education Association, the National PTA, the National School Public Relations Association, the National School Volunteer Program, and the American Association of School Administrators. Nurturing and appreciating school volunteers have become very important.

Houston, Texas. Just what a well-organized volunteer program can mean to a school system is exemplified in the sprawling, largely minority Houston, Texas, Independent School District. In 1979, Houston counted one school/business collaboration. By 1985, school officials could count 245 separate programs in 93 schools.

The commitment of the volunteers can be awe inspiring. The architects who fan out into 10 schools every semester for eight-week minicourses not only lecture on architecture but also help students build models of urban designs or evaluate how the space in their schools could be used more functionally. Hughes Tool sends 20 primarily blue-collar workers to three nearby schools to help non-English-speaking students in reading and math. When some of the tutors were laid off work because of economic decline, they continued to visit the schools and help the students. Moreover, many tutors visited the students' homes and celebrated birthdays with them.

"The effect on the morale of the workers is just as dramatic as on the students," commented the company's program manager.

IBM also makes a "people connection" with the Houston schools. Its personnel teach computer science to a dozen students from the individualized learning center one full day a week; last year's graduates all continued in computer science either in the workplace or at college. The company loans 22 professionals for regular tutoring at one elementary school, gives an internship to a handicapped student, and provides an engineer who teaches full time at a high school.

Another involved company in Houston is Tenneco which sends 20 volunteers into one high school each week while another 25 work with students on special projects. Tenneco also funds generous scholarships, and makes available summer jobs for 100 students; it also has been involved in such projects as the science fair, students-as-volunteers, and landscaping the school grounds.

Additional partners

Spokane, Washington. "A volunteer's job is no longer for the amateur," said Jack Clarcq, school board member and author of an article on volunteer programs for the New York State School Boards Association *Journal.* "No place is that more evident than in the public schools where a new view of the volunteer—one that stresses professionalism—is required of administrators, classroom teachers, and, yes, volunteers. Clarcq formulated his opinions after studying the Spokane, Washington, volunteer program which began in 1970 with 45 volunteers, many from the Junior League. Today, the district has 800 volunteers who give a minimum of a halfday per week to the schools: a ratio of one volunteer to every two teachers.

The district figures that monetarily it is the big winner in its volunteer program. It funds the central volunteer office with a salaried coordinator, publications, media advertising, and worker's compensation benefits for the volunteers, with a total cost to the district of about $32,000. The volunteers, meanwhile, provide 38,000 hours of service annually; at minimum wage, this amounts to $127,300 worth of service.

The school district has sustained its volunteer program, according to research by the state education department, because of:

- *District funding and support.* Just as support from the top sustains efforts in corporations, so the central administration in the Spokane schools provides moral and financial support to its volunteer efforts. This occurs while delegating ownership to neighborhood school units.
- *Neighborhood ownership.* Volunteer coordinators are selected by the community and "match" the social, economic, ethnic, and cultural qualities of the community. The coordinator, in turn, matches the needs of individual teachers with screened volunteers.
- *Consideration of school personnel.* Teachers receive volunteer help only if they request it, and the leadership of principals and teachers is stressed in the program literature, written agreements, and working operations. "It takes only one volunteer who wants to take over to create bad feelings about the volunteer program," says the Spokane coordinator. "We emphasize to volunteers that they must accommodate themselves to school rules, schedules, and leadership."
- *Balanced reward system.* The program equitably balances monetary and nonmonetary rewards. Volunteers receive ongoing education opportunities from teachers, workshops, invitations to faculty meetings, and training with new technologies, such as computers. These efforts help ease volunteers back into the job market if they wish. The program also stresses recognition and approval of volunteer work.
- *Professional standards.* Volunteers are carefully screened, given thorough orientation, and put on "probation" like other professionals.

In addition to these components of a successful program, Spokane's sponsors believe there are three variables critical to the program: flexibility and adaptability to the differing needs of individual schools, the candid treatment of suspicions between school personnel and volun-

Partnerships

teers, and the recognition that sufficient time must elapse for the program to build. Five to 10 years for development of such a program is not unreasonable, say Spokane organizers.

Successful volunteer programs can happen anywhere. They are not limited to large districts; the enthusiasm and vitality of individuals can be marshalled for the benefit of students in even the smallest of districts.

Hudson, Ohio. A case in point is the Hudson, Ohio, school district that for 17 years has depended on VIP—Vitally Interested People. "Schools can't buy what volunteers give," says Betty Berens, founder of VIP and now coordinator of the program for this 3,500-student school district. Hudson's volunteer program contributed to the designation of three of the district's five schools as exemplary by the U.S. Department of Education's national recognition program.

During the 1984-85 school year, 800 community volunteers donated 35,000 hours to the schools. The volunteer project, says Berens, has become an integral part of school and community life, enlisting people ages 10 to 90. VIP has become the umbrella for activities of all volunteer groups—PTO, Boosters, Jaycees, and others. VIP coordinators meet monthly with school administrators, relying on such personal contact rather than paperwork.

VIP volunteers must meet only two requirements: an interest in schools and a commitment to an agreed-upon amount of time. An extensive questionnaire makes it easy for volunteers to select exactly what they wish to do, and provides many suggestions for those uncertain what they might be able to offer.

Begun in the elementary schools, Hudson's VIP program has spawned several offshoots. One is the Hudson High School Student Volunteer Program, open to all students. In less than a year, this program, which provides opportunities for students to work in the community and thus return the favor of community volunteers, grew from five students to 90. Students have worked with Christmas food programs, driven people to doctor's offices and grocery stores, helped with meals at a nursing home, tutored younger students, welcomed new ones, shoveled snow, and helped at senior citizens meetings.

Salt Lake City, Utah. "Be a school drop-in." This is Salt Lake City's invitation to become part of one of the most successful and best organized school volunteer programs in the nation. Launched in 1969, primarily with local foundation funds, the nonprofit Salt Lake City Volunteers Inc. is headed by a volunteer board of about 30 local citizens and a full-time coordinator funded by the school district. It marshals and directs the training and involvement of more than 15,000 volunteers in the schools every year. Through coordinators at each school, provided by the PTA for the elementary schools and through district staff at the secondary schools, many programs help the schools and students in several ways, including:

- *SMILES.* This award-winning program is the Senior Motivators in Learning and Educational Services, for volunteers over 55. The citywide board hires a coordinator for this program which

Additional partners

arranges for help in the classrooms, offices, libraries, tutoring and special events. With the PTA, the board sponsors an Older Neighbor and Grandparents Day every October. Each spring SMILES volunteers and school coordinators are honored at a special recognition party.

- *Adopt-a-school.* Through school/business partnerships, employees are given released time to volunteer in schools. Church groups, civic groups, athletic teams, and fraternal organizations also are involved in this program. Retirees associated with these groups especially are encouraged to participate.
- *Basic skills.* Volunteers are given special preparation by board training programs to help in one-on-one tutoring in reading and math skills, as well as other subjects. Several tutoring programs are established at all school levels.
- *Public awareness committee.* This volunteer board helps develop awareness of the school volunteer programs throughout the district and community.
- *"Kid on the Block."* Primary Children's Hospital and the Salt Lake schools' pupil services department collaborate on providing volunteers for a troupe of puppets that help children become sensitive to the special feelings and concerns of handicapped people.
- *Salteens.* The volunteer board gives help and recognition to the thousands of students who volunteer each year as peer and cross-age tutors, library helpers, crossing guards, and school aides.

Skills from seniors

A hug here, a word of encouragement there, a chance to hear a personal story from the past or have one read aloud—all of these activities have become synonymous with senior citizens in the nation's classrooms.

Taking advantage of this rich resource for schools and students, the nonprofit Home and School Institute published a *Senior Corps Handbook* to help senior volunteers. It contains materials and suggestions for senior volunteers to use with children in grades 5 through 8 who need special skill help.

The enrichment activities are in reading, math, and health—all designed around topics that supplement regular classroom instruction. The handbook also suggests resources and activities that senior volunteers can send home with students to involve their parents in skill improvement.

The Home and School Institute
1201 16th St., NW
Washington, D.C. 20036

Partnerships

The board's volunteer activities gain substance through a well-organized training program that includes basic skills workshops and volunteer training; Effective Involvement of Volunteers, a college credit class for administrators and volunteers; and an annual statewide workshop for Salt Lake City volunteers and others throughout the state.

Other activities include "Mainstreaming the Handicapped," a five-week class for teachers and volunteers. Handbooks for principals, volunteers, coordinators, and teachers help each group integrate volunteer activities into the schools.

While organization and structure contribute to the success of the Salt Lake City program, it is the individual motivation and enthusiasm of the volunteers that truly makes it work. Says Ruth Muth, a retired teacher who decided to become a volunteer when she was 80 years old, "There are all these people who need you."

Higher education: Linkages between higher education and the public schools have great potential. . . .

In recent years, to the detriment of both, higher education and the public schools have stood somewhat estranged from each other. Except for student teaching arrangements, even colleges of teacher education have been accused of a certain aloofness to the everyday concerns of teachers and school systems.

Franklin Wilbur of Syracuse University points out that "given the historical development of our schools and colleges, differences in orientation and sense of mission, and vast differences in organizational climate, it is little wonder schools and colleges have grown apart and that truly collaborative activities are the exception rather than the commonplace."

Fortunately that picture is changing. In 1983 higher education officials and state education chiefs gathered at Yale University. Brought together by Ernest Boyer, president of the Carnegie Foundation, the group discussed and shared ideas on how higher education could develop cooperative programs with the schools.

As Wilbur further noted, "in communities throughout North America, a mutuality of purpose is being allowed with mutual respect, and the heavy penalizing chains of misunderstanding and mistrust are giving way. New links are being forged."

Some efforts have already begun (a few are detailed in Chapter 3 of this book), such as Syracuse University's Project Advance, offering college courses for credit in high schools taught by high school faculty, and the Yale-New Haven Teachers Institute. Elsewhere, through PREPS (Program of Research and Evaluation for Public Schools) at Mississippi State University, one research project benefiting all of the school districts in the university's consortium and one research project for each of the districts are undertaken each year. Indeed, the Yale meeting confirmed that much was happening, but that a great potential existed for much more.

In more than 20 cities, college and secondary school faculties are working together in the "county medical society" model, under the aus-

Additional partners

pices of the Urban University/Urban School Collaborative funded by the Exxon and Ford foundations through the National Association of State Universities and Land Grant Colleges.

For example, in Oakland, California, the University of California/Berkeley and the Oakland Unified School District are cooperating on a multi-year effort to improve mathematics education in the school district. It has led to significantly improved enrollment, retention, and achievement by minority students in college preparatory math; improved the management and communication between district administrators and teachers, and expanded into elementary grades and additional subject areas.

In Kansas City, the Metropolitan Area Schools Project provides a way for all superintendents in both the central city and suburban school districts (in Missouri and Kansas) to collaborate on projects with the University of Missouri/Kansas City as the facilitator. Districts cooperate on such projects as improved math and physics education, inservice teacher education, and research on applied methods of teaching course content.

Yale-New Haven Teachers Institute. Perhaps the project most talked about in recent years is the Yale-New Haven Teachers Institute. Although the university does not have a teacher education program, former Yale president A. Bartlett Giamatti believed his campus had an obligation to reach out and share its resources with the community around it. In 1978, the university began using its faculty members as partners with the teachers in the New Haven public schools.

Teachers became Fellows of the Teachers Institute, agreeing to attend talks and seminars, to conduct research, to prepare a curriculum, and to submit a written evaluation of the program. For the 80 teachers enrolled each year, the talks and seminars begin in March and continue through July. From April through July the teachers prepare a curriculum unit based on their studies at Yale; five to seven seminar topics in art, history, English, science, math, and other topics are offered each year. During the first five years of the project, teachers developed more than 300 curriculum units for the public schools based on these seminar classes. Studies of the project have shown it:
- Improved teacher preparation in their discipline
- Raised teacher morale
- Heightened expectations for students
- Encouraged teachers to remain in their profession
- Enhanced student performance.

The teacher fellows receive an honorarium of $650 upon completion of the Institute, but comments of participating teachers point to a value worth more than money: self-esteem. Treated as fellow teachers—with privileges at the university's libraries and use of other campus facilities and resources—the teachers come to regard themselves as fellow scholars.

The Teachers Institute has received support from the National Endowment for the Humanities and a number of foundations. Yale is seeking to raise a $4 million endowment fund to make the institute permanent.

Partnerships

VIP: Vitally Interested People supporting Hudson schools

Partnership between the school and community is what makes Hudson's school unique. Principals welcome volunteers into all buildings to help in 101 different ways. Among the ways suggested are:

____ At home: Make charts and games, sew, phone, etc.

____ Audiovisual: Tape record material and edit tapes.

____ Book Talks: Entice students to read selected books.

____ Chaperone: Field trips, dances, programs, etc.

____ Classroom Assistant: Help teacher in the classroom.

____ Clinic Mom: Give TLC to sick and hurt kids.

____ Computer Assistant: Help with computer-assisted instruction.

____ CPR: Teach CPR to students.

____ Eighth grade English publication: Type and proofread students' contributions for book.

____ Extracurricular advisor: Stamp Club.

____ Foreign cultures: Share culture with students. Specify _____

____ Gifted programs

____ Individual projects: Help students use library for individual projects.

____ Language lab: Supervise small groups of students.

____ Learning disability: Assist L.D. teacher.

____ Library: Check books, shelve, file, type.

____ Lunchtime: Supervise eating, activities.

____ Math Resource Center: Monitor material for teachers.

____ Nurse Assistant: Vision screening.

____ Offices: Copy, collate, phone, type.

____ Outdoor education: Nature study.

____ Picture Lady: Show and explain paintings to children.

____ SHARE: Teach about handicaps through puppets.

____ Skyrockets: Motor coordination activities.

Partial list from An Invitation to Become a School Volunteer, *Hudson, Ohio, schools*

Additional partners

New York Alliance. In the Empire State, a coalition of college deans, city school officials, and civic and community leaders constitutes a powerhouse of influence, the New York Alliance for the Public Schools, that works hard at finding substantive solutions for some of the most difficult problems school districts face.

Started in 1979 under the auspices of New York University, the alliance includes leadership from the New York City Board of Education, the United Federation of Teachers, the Council of Supervisors and Administrators, business and community representatives, and a consortium of deans from the City University of New York, Fordham University, New York University, St. John's University, and Teachers College at Columbia University.

The alliance focuses on what higher education institutions can do to help public education and seeks to strengthen the commitment of the business and professional communities to those schools. Among its projects have been:

- *Principal as curriculum leader.* Funded with a $430,000 grant from the Chase Manhattan Bank Foundation, this program included all of New York City's 111 high school principals as well as selected assistant principals. University faculty from the five participating campuses met with the principals in seminars, workshops, conferences, and consultations to help them with instructional supervision and curriculum development, and strategies for dealing with special students, teaching basic skills, and improving school management. The program established an ongoing network among the participating principals and identified assistants who would be good principal candidates.
- *MENTOR.* This project pairs each participating high school (22 in 1984) with a law firm. During daylong seminars at the schools, associates and partners from the law firm discuss the basics of the legal system. They also invite groups of students to tour the law firm, accompany them to federal and state courts, and meet judges and others in the court system. The lawyers informally discuss legal reasoning and law-related careers with students. The program has been adopted in Washington, D.C., Arizona, and Washington state, and plans are underway to expand it to include engineering, advertising, and careers in education.
- *COMPUTERLINK.* This is a data bank that lists more than 2,000 faculty members from the five participating universities who have volunteered to offer consultation to public school teachers and administrators. The fields represented by the faculty range from art, architecture, and archaeology to business, law, ethnic studies, and engineering.
- *Annual teacher awards.* With a $50,000 endowment from one of the original law firms in the MENTOR project, the public schools each year honor five teachers who exemplify high professional achievement. The cash awards are $1,000 each.
- *Mathematics and Science Recertification Program.* To help solve the critical shortage of math and science teachers, the participating universities developed a recertification program. Teachers already

Partnerships

certified in other fields may enroll tuition-free at colleges throughout the five boroughs of the city for 18 to 36 credits in math or science. The program arranges for them to take the licensing exam for a second certificate. In 1983-84 more than 500 teachers—many of whom were teaching math or science without a certificate—received college credit under this program.
- *Dropout research.* At the request of the chancellor of the New York City schools, the Alliance campuses undertook a study of high school dropouts.
- *Teaching the Three Rs: What Every Principal Should Know.* This is a series of workshops for elementary school principals on new research findings about the teaching of reading, writing, and arithmetic. More than 200 principals participated in the first round of workshops.
- *GO PUBLIC!* This privately funded public information campaign focuses on the range and diversity of academic, cultural, and vocational programs in the city's more than 900 schools. It began with market research on public attitudes toward the schools, then concentrated on encouraging parents to visit schools and making the corporate community aware of quality programs in many of the city's schools. The campaign included public service announcements, news conferences with the mayor, posters on buses, advertisements, and radio and television bookings.

At a meeting in the spring of 1985 to compare notes on these urban university/school partnerships, leaders from both constituencies agreed that early collaborations focused on top-level communication. For projects to endure, school principals need to be involved. Additionally, collaborations have focused on reform at the school level; a needed dimension is reform on the campuses, particularly regarding minority student retention and more effective rewards for university faculty involved with local school district projects.

Now that you've learned of the marvelous things beings done through partnerships in other school districts, it's time to start your own programs or revitalize existing ones. Chapter 5 will tell you how to get started.

Tips for foundation funding

Strengthening schools as institutions should be the focus of foundation funding, according to Theodore Lobman, program officer at the William and Flora Hewlett Foundation. Lobman suggests seven criteria for foundations to use in judging if proposals submitted to them will result in lasting change. They are:

- *Fit with district or school plans.* Have priorities been set and do the proposals reflect those priorities? Is the timing right? Are the districts prepared to share the costs?
- *Critical mass.* Enough teachers in a school should be participating in the project to sustain its momentum.
- *Stability.* Staff turnover can dilute the impact of a project, so foundations should look for personnel patterns indicating the participants in a program will continue to work together.
- *Adequate time.* Are proposed programs long enough?
- *Mix of pedagogy with subject matter.* Teachers learning new material also must be prepared to teach it. Do the proposals allow for practice teaching or peer assessments?
- *Follow-up.* Are there mechanisms to support teachers after they have been trained?
- *Evaluation in practice.* Does a proposal provide for deciding what teachers are doing differently after a program has ended?

In order to encourage schools to change, Lobman suggests foundations prod schools to set their own directions, help them create a culture of experimentation, break into the personnel system, encourage comprehensive partnerships with business and higher education, require matching support, and help states underwrite lasting quality in the schools.

Excerpted from State Education Leader, *Winter, 1985.*

Chapter 5

Lessons learned from partners

There are, as yet, no clear-cut formulas for success in developing school/community partnerships. As we have seen, in one year alone there were more than 46,000 such programs in place, and, even though they involved just 20 percent of school districts (but 80 percent of city districts), they differed so in scope and objectives that it is difficult to state categorically what works and what doesn't.

In fact, it is likely that what works for the urban East Coast school district isn't at all applicable to the small rural district in the farm belt. For one thing, the available resources aren't the same—not everyone has embassies to tap as do the District of Columbia public schools. On the other hand, the largest proportion of projects reported in a 1984 Department of Education survey was sponsored by small businesses, and nearly every school district has those.

Determining what succeeds and what fails in a partnership arrangement requires tracking for a sufficient length of time to determine how the dynamics work, points out Paul Barton, president of the National Institute for Work and Learning in Washington, D.C. Since partnership collaborations in any numbers are pretty much a phenomenon of the past decade, that kind of research is just beginning. Says Barton:

> Partnerships are being started all the time; they also are dying all the time. Often they stop when a specific objective is reached. Or they stop when a key individual leaves a firm or leaves a school system. Collaborative councils sometimes take root in a community and are sustained for decades. Others operate for a while and falter when the initial funding from government or a foundation comes to an end....

That doesn't sound particularly promising. What is encouraging is the conclusion of the Department of Education report that "most districts report such efforts to be on the increase and that such a variety of different activities and supports are being provided to our schools."

There are those who would underscore the need for partnerships in far more urgent terms. To wit:

> This is a fragile historical moment for public schools in general and especially for urban schools. In economic terms, there is no necessary reason for the business community to support public schools. When a manufacturer is dissatisfied with an existing queue of job applicants, the least certain and most cumbersome

Partnerships

response is to upgrade the skills of the entire pool from which only a few will be selected. Recent history demonstrates some other solutions: (1) move the operation to a better pool; (2) redesign the job to include robotics; (3) get out of hard-to-maintain, labor intensive businesses; and/or (4) buy education from an alternate, more "efficient" vendor.

Dale Mann, "All That Glitters: Public School/Private Sector Interaction in Twenty-Three Cities."

To Mann, school/business partnerships are essential if public schools and the private sector are to gain an understanding of and respect for each other. It is his belief that such a relationship is vital to the continuation of the public school system as we know it today.

Otherwise, he says, "The business community may well decide that the best policy involves 'breaking the monopoly of the public schools,' using the competition of a publicly funded, privately run set of alternate schools to improve education. The pressures for tuition tax credits and vouchers reinforce that... Unless the [current system] does a good job at the current generation of transactions, there may not be another."

Mann's doomsday predictions notwithstanding, a lot of school districts have found that partnership programs are good business and work for the betterment of the schools. That is reason enough to become involved. Moreover, sometimes the partnership actually pairs public and private institutions, instead of pitting them against each other.

For example, a New York City public high school and the Fieldstone School in the Bronx are joined in a project called Urban Arts, which brings students and teachers from both schools together for joint art classes and projects, including an arts festival. In St. Louis, Missouri, inner city schools and private elementary schools in more affluent parts of town arrange for students to do things together—take field trips, perhaps, followed by lunch.

In the Catholic Diocese of Philadelphia, whose 300 schools enroll a large percentage of the city's non-Catholic minority population, a business partnership—Business Leadership Organized for Catholic Schools (BLOCS)—was created according to the rationale that the graduates of all of a community's schools, public and private, represent the economic potential of the city. In fact, the organizers primarily were non-Catholics who believed the schools should have the support of the entire community. The archdiocese established a director's post and provided an office; the more than $23 million raised since 1980 has been used for capital improvements, curriculum, tuition assistance, and a scholarship endowment.

Partnership lessons: Don't reinvent the wheel. . . .

Not all partnerships run so smoothly as the parochial/public school collaboration in Philadelphia, of course. There are pitfalls; they exist in any worthy endeavor. Liability concerns, certification problems, and potential difficulties with the negotiated contract all may have to be

Lessons learned from partners

addressed, depending on the program design.

"But for too long we've looked at the barriers and said such things couldn't work," comments Nancy Turner, a consultant and former school administrator. "[Most] districts have found that if the effort is made to make them work, the payoffs are tremendous."

The preceding chapters with their litany of success stories certainly show that to be true. And there is another lesson to be learned here, besides the exhortation to jump in and get started. That is, quite simply: Don't reinvent the wheel.

In fact, that is the title of a short study by the Institute for Educational Leadership. After studying 10 school/business partnerships, the Institute concluded in its report, *Let's Not Reinvent the Wheel: Profiles of School/Business Collaboration,* that there is a partnership track record to be considered. While every community is different and must work with different resources (both economically and in its leadership), just about every idea for a partnership activity or policy has been tried somewhere, sometime. It just makes good sense to adopt someone else's program if applicable.

A sure BET from California partners

When the California Chamber of Commerce set out to promote school/business partnerships, there were more ideas about what to do than how to do it. A year later, these conclusions were reached by James Harper, director of Project BET (Business and Education Together):

- Commitment depends on the amount of planning, deadline setting, and coordination undertaken by a task-oriented group.
- School officials are interested primarily in long-term commitments from business.
- The credibility of a program is established or lost within its first few weeks.
- Educators ardently support partnerships that have significant impact on student performance.
- Once teachers undertake successful partnership activities in the classroom, they will often expand the effort to cover a substantial portion of their curriculum.
- The best way to gain media coverage is to concentrate on the local market.
- Those responsible for coordinating partnership programs should be key contact people from the sponsoring companies so that they can ensure that activities are sustained.

Harper's conclusions were reported in ProEducation *(April 1985).*

Partnerships

While the diversity of approaches was a hallmark of the partnerships studied by IEL, there were some common themes, among them:

- *There was an emphasis on skills.* Successful projects focused on three areas of essential skills: the basic skills of reading, writing, and math; job-finding skills such as interviewing and writing resumes; and on-the-job skills, including human relations, attitude, attendance, proper grooming, and working under supervision.
- *Size was no factor.* Projects of any size, from a collaboration between a small local business and a single school to citywide, or even state and national, programs can, and do, work.
- *Budgets cannot be overlooked.* Financial contributions may range from a few dollars to millions, but the important thing is to have a steady source of income to count on.
- *Key actors can vary.* Programs can be initiated and implemented by education, business, or even other interested third parties with no change in their success quotient. Often, one partner dominates over the other.
- *Commitment is paramount.* No project can be successful without the commitment of all involved, but especially the top leadership in both business and education.

Others who have either studied or experienced successful partnerships have developed their own checklists of what works and what doesn't.

Additional resources

The National Association for the Exchange of Industrial Resources finds and channels free industrial/corporate donations of equipment and materials. The donations are for educational and other nonprofit organizations.

This service can supply such items as science equipment and supplies, building maintenance supplies, office equipment, art prints, paper products, and computer diskettes. The merchandise is new and usually donated because of excess supplies.

Contact the exchange at P.O. Box 8076, 540 Frontage Road, Northfield, Illinois 60093. There is an annual fee for those who receive donations through NAEIR.

As part of a research project, Thomas Lee and Margaret Carr developed a manual, *Give and Take,* that covers Internal Revenue Service codes on the donation and acceptance of corporate gifts. Contact the American Association for Corporate Contributions, 800 Hillman Avenue, Suite 701, Evanston, Illinois 60202.

Lessons learned from partners

Partnering: From education's perspective....

As we have already seen in chapter after chapter, experienced school partners have a wealth of ideas on how to get started, how to keep the momentum going, and what pitfalls to avoid. We'll touch here on just a couple more.

Education Commission of the States. Lois Jackson of the District of Columbia schools, writing on partnerships for the Education Commission of the States, advises top school leadership to analyze the current and future job markets in the area. Then, she says, analyze the strengths and weaknesses of the schools and outline a pilot project that would fill a void and that could be accomplished by education and business working together.

Put together proposals that partners can help shape, she says. Consider those involving several partners, "thus diffusing risks and responsibilities and possibly increasing the staying power of the partners.

"Business will respond well," reminds Jackson, "to innovative proposals that combine courage with common sense."

She suggests a number of strategies for schools to adopt when developing such projects:

- *Acquire a mentor in the business community.* Seek out someone who knows the dynamics of your particular business community and can test your strategy, ideas, and priorities. Such a mentor is likely to introduce you to other business people. If your mentor is respected in the business world, the result is immediate credibility and easy access. To nurture these relationships, you must keep mentors informed and perform as promised.
- *Understand prospective partners before you contact them.* If you understand the motivations, priorities, and limitations of prospective partners, you will have a sound basis for communication.
- *Go straight to the top.* Approach the chairman of the board, the president, or a senior vice president. This may take more time at first, but it pays off in the long run.
- *Address the issue of quality at the outset.* Because business is concerned that students can graduate from high school without competencies in basic skills and thinking skills—and business seems to take a dimmer view of the work readiness of graduates than educators do—school leaders should emphasize the efforts schools already are making to improve educational quality.
- *Cite mutual benefits.* Point out that business has a vested interest in education. Emphasize equity problems and the new skills workers will need to meet the demands of a changing economy.
- *Allay fears.* Some businesses are fearful of dealing with the public sector. If a business wishes to maintain a low profile, honor that and assure your potential partners that you will keep them informed.
- *Downplay money.* Dispel the notion that you are proposing to fill the gap created by cutbacks in education budgets. Stress the value of in-kind education budgets and emphasize how much can be accomplished at the outset with expertise rather than just cash.

Partnerships

- *Provide examples.* Let potential partners know about other effective collaborations. "Reference-selling" is especially useful if the prospective partner is new to partnerships with schools.
- *Ask for a commitment.* Once you have laid out what you propose to do in a management plan that sets target dates, try to get an immediate commitment to begin working on the details with staff.
- *Be results-oriented, responsive, and timely.* Point out how the actions you propose directly affect children. Deliver what you promise, by the time you promise.

Partnering: From a businessman's perspective. . . .

Most of the program examples in this book address the dynamics of partnering from education's viewpoint. But there is no dearth of advice for business or community partners, and, in fact, it is often the local business that initiates such a partnership.

The Chamber of Commerce. In his guide, *Business and Education: Partners for the Future,* Robert Martin of the Chamber of Commerce of the United States lists how a local chamber can get started on a business/education partnership by asking a few questions:

- What can we do to better assist noncollege bound students?
Possibilities—Establish employment orientation courses. Work with guidance counselors to identify local employment opportunities. Provide work-study and cooperative education opportunities for students. Establish an award and recognition program for students.
- What can we do to serve students with special needs?
Possibilities—Establish academic enrichment courses, possibly instructed by business leaders in math, science, and computers. Create an education foundation that targets funds to special needs projects. Offer expanded work-study and cooperative education programs. Establish a partnership with a special needs program.
- How can we work together to ensure the funding needed for turning priorities into programs?
Possibilities—Work with community leaders to establish community awareness of the needs of public education. Support local school board candidates who are responsive to and reflective of business concerns. Work with statewide coalitions to influence education budget allocations, referenda, and elections.
- How do we assist the school system in rewarding and encouraging superior performance in teaching?
Possibilities—Support salary increases for outstanding teaching performance. Offer or support programs for scholarships, internships, and summer employment for teachers. Develop award and recognition programs.
- How do we make the business skills in the community available to the school system?
Possibilities—Establish a peer match program with local business and education leaders. Create a study group to study possible joint

Lessons learned from partners

ventures. Establish an award and recognition program to single out innovative management practices and cost savings.

West Hartford, Connecticut. "We're in this together," argues Peter Relic, superintendent of the West Hartford schools and a former federal education official. The "this" in his comment refers to better communities and schools. "We" refers to everyone interested in education, and that includes private and parochial schools as well as the public ones. Relic has helped to create partnerships between public and private schools in his area, tailored to the needs of students, teachers, and administrators.

For example, when the high schools decided they should offer Chinese studies, they applied together for a foundation grant. Students

---

Sustaining measures

Good management techniques can make business leaders more comfortable with their school partners. Lois Jackson, writing on collaborations for the Education Commission of the States, suggests these management tips:

- Management plans should be made for projects. Time schedules should be explicit, as should evaluation procedures.
- Goals, priorities, and schedules should be met jointly. Agreement should be reached about what constitutes success. Partners should establish formal checkpoints to identify what needs to be done; assign leadership responsibility; and choose business staff who can help coordinate the project, discuss progress, and readjust as needed.
- Communications should be ongoing and informal so that several matters can be resolved in a single phone call. Keep partners informed about developments and solicit opinions between formal checkpoints. Strive to minimize surprises.
- Use time efficiently. Schedule meetings far in advance; send reminders and preliminary agendas. Start meetings on time and keep them short. Be as succinct as possible in presentations; remember that proof is not as important initially as the feasibility of an idea and its potential benefits. Packaging proposals in executive summary format is often effective.
- Once you gain commitment, be ready to follow through. Be creative about breaking log jams within the educational structure—get the leaders involved to shorten turn-around time. Striking one partnership deal at a time makes sense, because you should deliver results as soon as possible after you have generated excitement.

Partnerships

from three high schools, including a private one, now attend classes in Chinese offered at just one of the schools.

West Hartford and parochial school teachers participate together in staff development courses offered in the public schools; West Hartford teachers have attended workshops on writing at a private school. Student councils from all area schools, including the American School for the Deaf, meet together regularly. Athletic and academic competitions include students from all the community schools. In return, private school leaders urge their parents to support the public school budget, emphasizing the community's common commitment to quality education.

Hudson, Ohio. Over a period of many years, the Hudson schools have developed a very comprehensive collaboration using community volunteers (see Chapter 4). On the basis of Hudson's experience, Betty Berens, program coordinator, has these suggestions for the continued vitality of a volunteer program:

- *Rely on the structured program.* That way, if there is a problem, "You'll know the basic reason is someone has not communicated right," instead of lack of organization.

If I were a superintendent again. . . .

"The first thing I would do is join actively any foundation or business education council that is established to improve schooling and make it clear that both elementary and secondary levels should be included. I would make a special effort within the school district and the entire community to speak and write often that a broad and general education is essential to the workplace. I would take the often-used words of corporate executives about the pivotal importance of general knowledge and skills to press home the enduring value to personal and career goals of the fine arts, humanities, and the sciences to any student leaving school for further education or the workplace. When I served as superintendent, this issue was not on my radar screen.

Second, I would be leery of any set of competencies developed by the business community until I had scratched the surface of corporate enthusiasm for non-specialized schooling. At face value, there may well be a conflict between a special interest group preparing an inventory of expected skills and the multiple goals of schooling. I would inspect carefully what those business scripted competencies are. My impulse would be to have corporate managers join parents and educators in creating skills rather than have one group do it alone. The fear I would have is that the competencies would be dressed-up versions of previously produced lists of narrow skills directed to those occupations where labor

Lessons learned from partners

- *Provide accountability and evaluation.* Berens knows exactly what the volunteer program costs and what is it worth (the cost to the school district is about two cents per volunteer hour). Evaluation is built into the Hudson program and starts anew each year.
- *Dispel the myths about volunteerism.* One such myth is that "people have time to give." Not so, says Berens. A volunteer has to choose, has to give up something else to work in the schools. Another myth is that volunteers work for free. "Volunteers get their own special paycheck," she notes. "It is the gut-level satisfaction of feeling good every time they leave the school building, not just at a ceremony at the end of the year." Volunteers need to feel appreciated—all the time.
- *Educate the volunteers.* They must know all they need to know about the schools, keeping in mind that the best recruiters for more volunteers "are satisfied customers."

American Council on Life Insurance. One of the most useful sources of information for businesses on developing collaborations with schools was prepared, with the help of the St. Louis, Missouri, schools, by the American Council of Life Insurance (ACLI) for its member companies.

---

demands currently run high. Schools need no further intensifying of vocationalism.

Third, I would exploit the splendid opportunity offered by corporations interested in expanding classroom and curricular efforts in thinking skills, problem-solving, or similar sounding phrases. Without getting into the complexities of this innocent but potent phrase, I believe the present focus on comprehension, analysis, and other complex intellectual skills including creative problem-solving, has captured one of the critical areas that schools are weakest in and desperately need intensive help from both the university and corporate sources.

"... Beyond these modest moves, I would be skeptical of the enthusiasm and rhetoric surrounding corporate involvement in schools. Moderation in striking a balance between conflicting purposes of schools, insistent demands of various constituencies, and professional judgments about what's best for students remains the quintessential task facing school policymakers. Such a balance among parents, professionals, taxpayers, and business firms' agendas is called for now especially when a catchy melody is played by corporate players."

Larry Cuban, Stanford University, and former superintendent in Arlington, Virginia. Excerpted from a paper prepared for the National Institute of Education and the American Enterprise Institute.

Partnerships

Both partners must respect each other as professionals, avers ACLI. And both groups must agree on a common set of principles before the partnership begins. Other points in the manual suggest that:

- Commitment from company leadership is essential. The chief executive officer's support is absolutely necessary; the more directly the CEO is involved, the greater the chances for success.
- On education's side, support from the individual school's principal is equally important. Of course school board approval must be sought, but without the involvement of the principal, programs in schools just don't work.
- Both parties must accept the premise that the ultimate goal of the collaboration is to improve education for all students. Nothing must interfere with that objective, even though individual projects may have a more limited target audience.
- Programs need not follow established patterns as long as they meet mutually agreed upon goals.
- Planning should include representatives from the company and the school. Schools should include companies in their long-term planning and companies should conceive of their efforts as part of that long-term plan.
- Both parties should agree that the collaborative effort be given time to develop.
- Honesty and flexibility should characterize each interchange between partners. Schools should be realistic about what business can provide and open to new approaches. Companies should be straightforward about the extent of the resources they will commit and sensitive to the realities of schools today.

The ACLI's *Manual for Developing Successful Projects* also tells of pitfalls to avoid:

- Realize that schools do not and cannot operate like businesses.
- Look at your participation as something more than a means of recruiting potential employees.
- Stay away from publicity gimmicks.
- Promise only what you can deliver, and be realistic about the results you can expect.
- Plan to make a contribution that is something more than financial.
- Stick with your program when it runs into the inevitable rough spots.

Before embarking on a partnership, the degree of commitment must be ascertained and, according to ACLI (and others experienced in such partnerships), that commitment must come from the highest levels of the company. In fact, this support is cited as the single most important factor in determining the success of a project.

Chief officers, ACLI notes, can determine the company's level of commitment, authorize use of company resources and assign a corporate officer to the program, enthusiastically promote company participation, and support means of rewarding employee participation.

Lessons learned from partners

It is not surprising, then, that research on partnerships finds top school leadership communicating directly with top corporate leadership in order to get such collaborations going. Furthermore, this kind of personal leadership sets the tone for the partnership.

If there is one common lesson throughout the insights gained through school/business partnerships, it is that the partners must bring the same dedication to the relationship that would be required of a genuine adoption or marriage or business partnership, concludes researcher Richard Lacey. "The process requires time, it requires knowledge, it requires top level commitment, it requires systematic management by people who can operate well in both worlds."

Successful partnerships are like a family, he continues. Such a collaboration cannot be legislated. Rather, "it comes about as a result of a partly fortuitous, partly designed set of circumstances and commitments of people (at) the right time, the right place."

The Conference Board. William Woodside is president of the American Can Company, a trustee of Barnard College and of the Committee for Economic Development, and a volunteer at the Martin Luther King Jr. High School in New York City. He believes that "a first-rate system of public education is every bit as important to our future as our national defense system."

In a speech delivered at a New York conference on new business initiatives in education, sponsored by The Conference Board, Woodside articulated his belief that a more global approach to school/community partnerships should replace individual, piecemeal projects.

> ...(W)e are now at the stage where we need to look beyond our individual partnership programs. We now need to focus on systemwide issues because there are vast and fundamental improvements that must be made in our public schools. And we need to focus on the political arena because that is where the major decisions are going to be made about the funds, priorities, and programs that will make or break our system of education.
>
> In the long run, the eventual success of today's business/school partnerships... will depend upon the impact that we have on the decisions that are made in our state capitals and in Washington as well as in our city halls.
>
> For us to be effective, it will mean more than telling our lobbyists to put in a good word for education... more than sending a corporate executive to Washington or Albany for an occasional visit....
>
> It will mean building coalitions that see major and permanent improvements in such areas as teacher training and certification, salaries, educational standards for students, and special programs for the disadvantaged. It will mean actively acknowledging that good schools... will require more of our time, take more of our efforts, and cost more of our money.

Woodside suggested several alternatives for business involvement at the national level, such as institutionalizing concerns by working through corporate legislative representatives, working through trade associations, or—the only solution he considers truly viable—forming

Partnerships

ad hoc corporate coalitions in Washington and state capitals.

"Ad hoc coalitions exist, and are effective, in such areas as health care, industrial growth, tax reform, and international trade," he said. "Why not action coalitions for public education" to bring to life some of the recommendations of existing studies, push for equitable funding in public education, and take concerted effort on issues relating to the professionalization of teachers?

Dayton-Hudson Corporation. One business partner with considerable experience to share is the Dayton-Hudson Corporation of Minneapolis, Minnesota, whose Dalton Bookstores were the centers of outreach organization around a PBS series, *Your Children, My Children,* which it helped to fund.

Partnerships must have the right environment, says Peter Hutchinson, Dayton-Hudson vice president of public affairs, including a community vision, networking, communication, and continuity. Hutchinson offers these comments about seven components for partnership success his company has identified:

- *Focus.* Partnerships work best if they are developed for a very specific reason. Be clear about why you're doing it and what you hope to accomplish.
- *Have a vision*—a shared dream about what the partnership is going to do.
- *Never resist a generous impulse.* Bring in anybody who shares the vision and wants to work. Partnerships are not exclusive clubs.
- *Seek progress, not perfection.* Celebrate small victories and don't condemn small failures. You'll have plenty of both.
- *Choose commitment over efficiency.* At Dayton-Hudson, we're willing to sacrifice a pint of efficiency to get a gallon of commitment.
- *Leverage whenever possible.* Get the most out of every resource available.
- *Build trust.* Trust holds the partnership together through rough spots. Lack of it is a major cause of partnership failures.

National Commission for Employment Policy. From a research viewpoint, Richard Lacey, in a project for the National Commission for Employment Policy, developed a thesis that "the sustained vitality of a partnership reflects the quality of trust developed at all levels of the collaborating organizations." He found three complementary themes in all successful partnerships:

- *Personal commitment and involvement.* The ongoing, visible, and personal commitment from top level corporate executives determines how well a partnership matures.
- *Networking.* Where there is effective communication, Lacey says, commitments to partnerships develop rather than level off or decline over time. Networks develop in individual schools and across several schools with partnership activities. When the collaboration occurs throughout a metropolitan area, informal as

Lessons learned from partners

well as official exchanges of views among corporate executives and public sector leaders lead to strategies for the whole community, such as improving public confidence in the schools or solving youth unemployment.

• *Systematic management of program planning and start-up.* Lacey examined school/business partnerships in five urban school districts and found widespread use of the National School Volunteers Program (NSVP) training for newly appointed corporate program coordinators whereby they developed and managed programs according to the stages set forth by NSVP. These stages include development of awareness, needs assessment, setting program goals, defining objectives, identifying potential resources, designing the program, implementing the program (recruitment, orientation, training, assignment, retention, and recognition), and evaluation.

Setting up YOUR program: Nuts and bolts advice from those who already have been through it. . . .

Researcher Paul Barton suggests the best approach to initiating partnership programs may be simply to follow the formation and development of several in communities similar to yours, or with similar objectives to what you hope to accomplish, and study those elements that have made them successful. That is our advice as well. Visit a district or two if possible. At the very least, contact the program coordinator or the superintendent by telephone. Most districts are more than willing to share successful programs: What someone else has learned can prevent your district from making their mistakes and can provide you with the kind of helpful advice needed to enter partnerships with sufficient information to make them work.

In the remainder of this chapter, we'll cull through some of the programs highlighted elsewhere in this book and share their advice for program structure, establishing working relationships, marshalling enthusiasm from both partners, and providing evaluation and rewards. More detailed examples and reproductions of actual documents used are provided in a special exhibits section to follow.

Here, then, are the steps to take in developing a partnership:

• **Pledge commitment.** Every researcher, every partner echoes this advice: without a real commitment from the leadership of all partners involved, the program hasn't a chance at long-term success. This commitment might involve a formal pledge, such as a school board resolution or a joint statement of purpose similar to the one that governs the Parker Pen project in Parker, Wisconsin: "to create and maintain in Wisconsin the finest, most skilled, best educated, work force in America. . . ."

There also must be commitment at another level, a real sense of dedication to the concept that partnerships are beneficial for education and that is important for the well-being of society. This is the sense of purpose that will overcome the problems that are inevitable and main-

Partnerships

tain momentum even when results aren't as positive as hoped for. And this commitment, experienced partners say, must come from the top leadership: the CEO and superintendent and their mutual boards. A program can be initiated by someone else, but it must gain the support of top leadership for strength and viability.

This commitment must recognize that partnerships take time and nurturing. One estimate is that 10 years are required for a partnership to become a working part of the educational system. Rita Kaplan of Honeywell Inc. expresses it this way: "The trouble with partnerships . . . is that you really have to keep working at them.

"I do not think that teachers who have been isolated from business really know how to use our resources, and we do not know what resources we have that they can use. We obviously need more communication. As we learn what each other's needs are, we will see complementary elements, the areas of common domain, and the contributions the other can make. This. . .takes a long time."

Patience is a corollary of the time requirement, for the building of a partnership requires healthy measures of both. It takes time for representatives of the various sectors to develop trust and understanding of one another. The implementation of partnership goals requires the support of all the people on which they will potentially impact. It takes sustained and patient effort to build that support.

- **Find outside partners.** They're all around you, waiting to be asked. Researcher Dale Mann found that much of what is being developed through partnerships began with the initiative of superintendents (as contrasted with other studies) rather than chief executive officers. Most superintendents took on the job of developing liaisons with the business community, often lamenting that school boards no longer have the stature or inclination to be the broker. Mann also found that teacher union leaders and school business managers are neither very knowledgeable of nor very involved in the partnership effort.

In about half the cities he studied, Mann found the partnerships contributed to what seemed to be long-term political alliances for more adequate public school support, creating a challenge to maintain the alliances while preserving the purposes of public schools.

In Murfreesboro, Tennessee, the Rutherford County board sends a letter, signed by the superintendent as well as the program coordinator, to selected "community leaders" asking them to consider the adopt-a-school program. The letter points out that this is not simply a means of raising funds "but rather to take advantage of the many resources in and around schools that we think can be profitably used to better educate children." A long list of possible activities is included—everything from resource speakers, career days, and field trips to assisting in school beautification, allowing murals to be drawn on company walls by art students, and sponsorship of a science fair. There are also activities listed that can benefit the targeted business. This last enclosure is important.

"It is not a partnership," Peter Hutchinson, vice president of public affairs for the Dayton-Hudson Corporation, told a San Diego, California conference on partnerships, "if you come to me and say, 'I've got this great idea—why don't you fund it?' If I have no interest in it, no

Lessons learned from partners

stake in its success, it won't work. I might do it, but it won't be a partnership. Nor is it a partnership if I come to you and tell you how to run your project because I've got the money and, therefore, think I'm smarter than you."

Private-public partnerships "are ventures that combine the complementary responsibilities and resources of business, government, community agencies, and foundations to meet a community need. Each partner brings resources. Each expects to benefit."

Consultant Nancy Turner counsels school districts to think first about what schools can do for business. "It's a two-way street," she admonishes, adding that the options are many, indeed.

For example, in one district, the schools loaned a guidance counselor and staff development person to a local business one summer to set up career counseling and staff development there. An early morning workout site in a school gymnasium for business and school personnel alike helped mental and physical juices flow in another district. Schools that have computer equipment and audio/visual equipment to loan can be of invaluable assistance to small businesses (in one district, the local social service agency uses school equipment to show training films to prospective foster families). One school librarian surveyed local businesses to determine what kinds of management books their people needed. She then alerted school management people when these were available.

When seeking partners, often it's a good idea to secure a mentor, as mentioned above, or at least someone whose advice the prospective CEO respects, to serve as icebreaker and on-site reference. And don't limit your horizons to local businesses. Excellent partnerships can be formed between schools and nonprofit organizations and institutions, such as hospitals, the Junior League, foundations, and more.

A final note: While it makes sense to try to match partners according to shared needs and goals—for example, a magnet school in journalism with the local newspaper—company/school proximity may be more important because it allows the ease of access that enables school and business people to get to know and appreciate each other. They also will share a mutual concern for the well-being of the neighborhood.

- **Drum up staff interest.** A partnership is sure to flounder without enthusiastic support from staff. In Hudson, Ohio, for example, volunteers help only those teachers who have requested it, and principals are totally involved in the planning and decision making. In Lancaster, New York, teachers in "adopted schools" receive a form with space for them to list suggested school needs, specific classroom needs, opportunities for new activities, and project ideas. It is suggested that teachers peruse the school's adopt-a-school manual, with its samples of other successful activities, to "get your own thoughts going." A similar form is distributed to appropriate employees at the adopting business. This exercise in exploring interests can be an important step in stimulating discussions and establishing trust.

Corporate coordinators in particular often underestimate the demands that a good partnership makes on employees' time and energy. Inexperienced coordinators should participate in sharing and learning

Partnerships

sessions with experienced people in other companies. They also should make sure their responsibilities and time allotment are defined in writing.

It may be easier initially to meet with one or two principals and secure their interest and commitment rather than attempting to implement a program systemwide. Both groups must be aware of basic attitudinal differences that will have to be resolved. Business is often skeptical of the schools' ability to train students for the world of work; education's emphasis on theoretical concerns also is difficult for business people to understand. Educators often have equal trouble with business' emphasis of practical over intellectual pursuits. The mentor or some sort of partnership broker (chamber of commerce director comes to mind) can help in bringing each side closer to understanding the other's needs and positions.

Beyond adopt-a-school

Partners in Education is the common sense way that the school system, city government, and business leaders in Hammond, Indiana, are working together to expand educational opportunities, promote economic development, and improve the community's quality of life.

Initiated by Hoosiers for Economic Development (HED), it is patterned after a program that has been operating successfully in Indianapolis for years.

For example, explains Margaret Dwyer, director of HED, there was one large company in Indianapolis that was overwhelmed with computer data and didn't have the staff to organize or analyze it. A high school science teacher with his advanced computer class moved in for a semester, wrote the necessary software, analyzed the data, and presented professional scientists with the results.

Both partners came out ahead: The company completed an important project without hiring additional staff, while the students designed and carried out a necessary task in an actual work setting.

"This is not an adopt-a-school concept," says Raymond Golarz, assistant superintendent in the Hammond City Schools. "That idea is 10 years behind the times."

Partners in Education, he adds, makes it mutually advantageous for business and the school system to cooperate.

"It's got to be a bottom-line issue," he says.

From a local newspaper article

Lessons learned from partners

- **Announce that a partnership has been formed.** Do this in whatever way you normally advise the media of new programs, either through a news release, a press conference, or a direct call to media contacts. Have photo opportunities or photographs already available and provide plenty of background information on the partnership movement (including examples of similar programs that have been successful—particularly useful if they are located in your state or region).

  When announcing a partnership, make sure you have the permission of all those involved. Most businesses relish the opportunity for "free" public relations, but some prefer anonymity. When planning the PR campaign, don't neglect the chamber of commerce newsletter, the business partner's house organ and internal school district publications, the state education department newsletter, and communiques sent home to parents in the affected school(s). The bad news always gets media attention—it's up to you to get as much coverage as possible for the "good news."

- **Create adoptor/adoptee council.** A formal organizational structure gives the partnership effort added credibility and stability. This might be a single advisory group or a plethora of committees such as in Fairfax County, Virginia, where there are four committees involved in some way with outside partnerships: the superintendent's business/industry advisory council, the vocational education advisory committee, the marketing and distributive education advisory board, and the business education advisory committee.

  Sometimes, partnerships become affiliated with already established groups, such as the education committee of the chamber of commerce or a local business council.

  In order to be viable, the partnership must have community support. An advisory committee is one means of involving outside people, even those not concerned with an immediate partnership project. Sometimes, the partnership council can address a community need and then enlist the support of business interests; other times the committee is formed after a collaboration relationship has been agreed upon. However it works in your district, follow your own district's procedures for establishing such a group.

  One expert suggests that the partnership should see itself linked to other community organizations and begin to make those links visible. "Staying sensitive to local political realities, for example, can make the difference between a partnership that survives and one that does not. Partnerships that fare best are those that demonstrate neutrality and responsiveness to diverse interests."

- **Charge council with joint planning.** This is where long and short range goals will be formulated, with a particular emphasis on the long range outlook. Researchers recently have focused their attention on the need for planning educational programs with farsighted vision.

  American Can Company President William Woodside is among those supporting a broader, more organized effort on behalf of public educa-

Partnerships

tion. In doing so, he says, he does not mean to minimize "what we have achieved in the past or trivialize the effort that has gone into establishing the partnerships we now have ... these initial programs generated a remarkable outpouring of personal involvement and commitment ..." but we need to have a broader perspective because it is the "decisions of Congress and the Executive Branch (that) set the tone for the nation as a whole. And we need to play an activist role in state capitals because they are becoming new centers of power in determining the level of financial and programmatic support our public schools will enjoy."

Echoing this advice for a more global perspective is Dale Mann of Columbia University. "Virtually everything that is now being done is project-based, i.e., episodic, special purpose, tacked on, and usually at the periphery of the school's core technology of teaching and learning," Mann concluded after studying school/business partnerships in 23 major cities. "That is a short leash for the schools and a fragile base for long-term partnerships." The small projects do some good, he concedes, but fall short of the potential that linkages offer.

A good advisory council can avoid these pitfalls; it certainly should set the tone and the scale for what the school district and the outside partner(s) hope to accomplish.

- **Establish actual programs.** As we've seen, there's no end to variety here. The specific projects selected will vary according to the needs, the demographics, and other specific circumstances of the community.

For example, one community might be switching from a rural to a more suburban, service-oriented economy where business growth, in the form of shopping malls, restaurants, fast food outlets, and places of lodging, is proceeding at a pace that taxes the available trained employee pool. A school/business collaboration that involves career counseling and actual vocational training in the service sector (including, but not limited to, operation of an actual restaurant facility at a local high school) is one option here.

Studying other programs is one of the best first steps in analyzing what kinds of programs to implement; involving creative people from within the school and without in the planning process is another.

If funding is an issue, it needs to be addressed here, but most partnerships flourish best when schools plan programs that go beyond the handout mentality.

Finally, keep in mind that intermediaries might be needed to get the ball rolling. Business people often are reluctant to take the lead in making program suggestions for fear of seeming to intrude, while school personnel may feel intimidated by their business peers.

- **Assign responsibilities among adopters/adoptees.** There should be clear-cut lines of responsibility so everyone knows exactly what is expected of him and what the limits are. To become useful programs, ideas need structure. Do all of the usual and necessary steps to provide that structure—set policies, appoint a coordinator, establish internal procedures, set a budget, and so on.

However, keep in mind the nature of the partners involved. They're likely to be disparate in their approach to process and will respond best

Lessons learned from partners

to a system that allows for flexibility, stresses openness, and can respond to initiatives quickly.

Establishing actual job descriptions might be important. Certainly it is if a program coordinator is designated. Some examples are included in the appendix. Keep in mind that school and business coordinators should be individuals who are "sold" on the concept, can motivate colleagues to participate, and who can work effectively with people of differing viewpoints. The motivation and leadership abilities of the coordinators will be crucial to the program's success.

● **Recruit volunteers from school/outside partner organization.** If you have done a good job of involving staff from the very beginning, recruitment of volunteers may not even be necessary—they'll be knocking down your doors to get started. This is true except in programs that will be based on volunteers from the community, such as parents and retired persons.

A way to begin the recruitment process is to encourage a group of interested business people to visit the school and arrange for a reciprocal visit by school staff. Remember that educators and business people can have a hard time understanding one another at first. Trust develops gradually through regular and nonthreatening interaction. Activities involving redefinitions of traditional roles, responsibilities, and "turf" should be planned when the trust level is high.

A major change in leadership or other circumstances, such as a strike or major layoffs, can affect the viability of a program and may require renewed commitment and recruitment efforts.

● **Orient volunteers.** Most programs have some sort of training procedure to help volunteers unfamiliar with schoolhouse routines and the dynamics of teaching. This might include an orientation session, brief teaching seminars, and/or on-site observation. Printed materials, such as handbooks or manuals, are important for maintaining communication.

Communication is the key to success with volunteers. From the Hudson, Ohio, schools' VIP program come these suggestions which are included in a handbook provided to each teacher who will be working with volunteers:

—Don't assume anything—the natural way of doing something may be what you want or *don't* want. The VIP is there to assist the teacher—YOUR way.
—Explain how to handle special situations, such as special student needs, fire drills, building procedures, and regulations.
—Set up a regular schedule for conferences to compare notes.
—Stress commitment on the part of the volunteer. Explain that students are counting on the VIP for special help.
—If the VIP is not suited to the job, suggest a school or type of job that will better use the VIP's abilities and then call the (program coordinator), so he can contact the VIP.

● **Show appreciation of volunteers.** While volunteers all receive some intrinsic rewards for what they are doing—whether it be the smile on a student's face or a sense of having done "good works"—they need con-

Partnerships

stant nurturing from program coordinators and others who benefit from their assistance. Too often people simply forget to say "thank you." Or, having said it once, they forget that it sounds just as good a second or third time.

Some school systems with large volunteer programs have newsletters just for this purpose. Advisory committees of key workers also can keep the message alive. Be generous with the recognition. Ceremonies are fine, but recognition should be an ongoing process, not just a tea and certificate at the end of the year.

● **Publicize program to community.** Once the partnership is underway, keep attuned to opportunities for future news coverage. The size of your community will determine to some extent how much coverage the local media will grant you: Small town papers generally devote more space to school activities (as distinct from education news of a more politically oriented nature) than do metropolitan ones.

This coverage is important: Not only does it serve as another means

---

Mutual benefits

Experienced partners always make the point that collaborations work only if there are mutual benefits for both or all parties involved. In his survey of partnership program, Paul Barton, president of the National Institute for Work and Learning in Washington, D.C., found that benefits vary with the type of partnership.

Even the same undertaking will mean different things to different sponsors, he notes. For one school adoptor, the benefit may be to identify the business as a good citizen in the community. Another may believe that by helping to improve student achievement, the company will benefit at the hiring office. Here are just some of the benefits he found:

For corporations
● Better understanding by young people of how the economy works and more appreciation of the private enterprise system
● A better educated workforce
● An improved image for the corporation
● More social stability in neighborhoods where corporations produce or sell
● Better informed consumers and voters
● Lower costs when relocating in a state that provides free training to attract business

Lessons learned from partners

of nurturing and rewarding participants (companies and individuals frequently like their names and photos to appear in the newspaper or on TV in a positive light) but it also is a recruitment device for other businesses and organizations that would like to collaborate with the schools.

- **Evaluate program.** If a concerted effort is not made to evaluate progress, the project eventually will falter. This is the point at which partners decide if what they have been doing is having a positive impact. Perhaps the project is not being run as efficiently as possible; perhaps additional funding sources need to be found; perhaps key people have left their positions and replacements should be sought. Formal structures, up to and including evaluation, allow programs to proceed in an orderly fashion. Evaluation also allows documentation of results which can be used to secure community support, additional partners, and continuing board sanction. The continuity of such programs over a period of years depends on it.

- Vocational school training that more nearly matches what employers need, and on equipment similar to what employers use
- Employee satisfaction from working with a company that does good things for communities
- Bottom-line results in terms of productivity and product quality resulting from education and training improvements.

For education
- A broadened base for the support of an education system that is blamed increasingly for student shortcomings
- Greater recognition of schools and what they contribute to business and the economy
- Financial resources
- Business people willing to come into the schools and help educate students about careers and training needs
- Access to expensive, state-of-the-art equipment
- Help with management problems
- Support for appropriations and school bond drives
- Experience for students that places priority on the role of experience in learning
- Use of employer facilities and personnel for student instruction
- Access to employers for job placement of graduates
- Alternatives for imparting basic skills to students who are hard to teach in traditional settings.

Exhibits

Exhibit #	Subject	Page
1	Additional reading	93
2	Helpful organizations	94
3	Sample pledge of commitment	95
4	Sample letter to recruit partners	96
5	Checklist for potential partners	97
6	School activities that benefit business	99
7	Samples of successful activities	100
8	School needs assessment form	102
9	Business/community volunteer interest form	104
10	Sample partnership council organizational chart	105
11	A large city's partnership plan	106
12	A student banking program	110
13	How a school helped a business	112
14	Sample job descriptions for partners	114
15	Sample volunteer interview form	117
16	Sample corporate volunteer application form	118
17	Sample volunteer orientation program	119
18	Sample public relations plan	121
19	Evaluation questions	122
20	Evaluation form for school staff	123
21	Evaluation form for corporate staff	124

Exhibits

Exhibit 1. Additional reading

1. *Business and Education: Partnership for the Future,* Chamber of Commerce of the United States, 1615 H Street, N.W., Washington, D.C. 20062.

2. *Company-School Collaboration: A Manual for Developing Successful Projects,* American Council of Life Insurance, Educational Services, 1850 K St., N.W., Washington D.C. 20006.

3. *Creating and Managing a Corporate School Volunteer Program,* National School Volunteer Program, Inc., 701 North Fairfax St., Alexandria, Va. 22314.

4. *Investing In Our Children: Business and the Schools,* Committee for Economic Development, 477 Madison Ave., New York, N.Y. 10022.

5. *Let's Not Reinvent the Wheel: Profiles of School/Business Collaboration,* Institute for Educational Leadership, 1001 Connecticut Ave., N.W., Washington, D.C. 20036.

6. *The Private Sector in the Public School: Can It Improve Education?,* American Enterprise Institute, 1150 17th St., N.W., Washington, D.C. 20036.

7. *Pro-Education,* a quarterly publication on partnerships in education; 5000 Park St. North, Petersburg, Fla. 33709.

Partnerships

Exhibit 2. Helpful organizations

American Association of School Administrators
1801 N. Moore Street
Arlington, Va. 22209

Chamber of Commerce of the United States
1615 H Street, N.W.
Washington, D.C. 20062

Education Commission of the States
Suite 300, 1860 Lincoln Street
Denver, Colo. 80296

Institute for Educational Leadership, Inc.
1001 Connecticut Ave., N.W.
Washington, D.C. 20036

National Alliance of Business
1015 15th Street, N.W.
Washington, D.C. 20005

National Association for Industry-Education Cooperation
235 Hendricks Blvd.
Buffalo, N.Y. 14226

National Community Educational Association
119 N. Payne Street
Alexandria, Va. 22314

National School Public Relations Association
501 Lee Highway
Arlington, Va. 22209

National School Volunteer Program
701 N. Fairfax Street
Alexandria, Va. 22134

Partnerships Data Net
1015 18th Street, N.W., Suite 300
Washington, D.C. 20036

White House Office of Private Sector Initiatives
The White House
Washington, D.C. 20500

Exhibit 3. Sample pledge of commitment

Recognizing the interdependence of the Shawnee Mission School District and the community it serves and the interrelatedness of education, social services, business, and industry, the Shawnee Mission Board of Education endorses and encourages the cooperative development of mutually beneficial partnerships. School-community partnerships shall be characterized by a sharing of skills and resources to achieve mutually identified goals and objectives designed to enhance the quality of education and the life of the community.

The district administration is hereby charged with the development of appropriate procedures and strategies for the successful implementation of mutually beneficial school-community partnerships.

Source: Shawnee Mission School District
Shawnee Mission, Kansas

Partnerships

Exhibit 4. Sample letter to recruit partners

Dear Community Leader:

The_____Schools would appreciate your consideration of a program we feel has been very successful in other areas. It is called adopt-a-school. This is a contractual arrangement between a business or an organization and one of our schools. Experience in other systems has shown that this type of arrangement can be advantageous to both parties. The adopt-a-school program is not a relationship designed to raise funds but rather to take advantage of the many resources in and around schools that we think can be profitably used to better educate children.

We feel that our county needs this type of partnership. Certainly, the economic growth and success of our county is dependent upon having good public schools available to any and all persons in the community. If your organization has locations elsewhere, you may already be familiar with the program.

If you feel that you would be interested in the possibilities, we would like the opportunity to discuss this further. We feel that it has great potential for our community. We'll look forward to hearing from you soon.

    Adopt-a-School Program   Superintendent
            Director

Source: Rutherford County Board of Education
Murfreesboro, Tennessee

Exhibit 5. Checklist for potential partners

The best way to find out if a business would be interested in becoming a partner to a school is to ask. If the local chamber of commerce is committed to developing stronger ties between businesses and schools, the chamber may be willing to do the asking.

The following checklist will help identify the specific interest areas or resources that a particular business may have. Based on the results, schools could then be matched appropriately with a "partner."

CHECKLIST

_____ Yes, our business would like to explore a full school partnership.
_____ Our business would like to explore a school partnership on a limited basis. We could lend support in the following ways:

FOR STUDENTS

_____ Provide classroom speakers and presenters. Host tours through our workplace.
_____ Arrange career "shadowing" of our employees for a day.
_____ Serve as a resource for a school-sponsored "Career Day" presentation.
_____ Arrange for student internships/mentorships so young people can learn our business first-hand.
_____ Serve as volunteer classroom tutors on a limited weekly basis.
_____ Consult with students involved in business-oriented research.
_____ Provide student scholarships.
_____ Allow students to help with company-involved community projects.
_____ Display student projects at your business (e.g., arts, crafts, photography, etc.).
_____ Hire students during summer or after school.
_____ Provide one-on-one counseling/training related to careers and job interviews.
_____ Allow students to give entertainment performances at our workplace.

FOR TEACHERS

_____ Serve as curriculum consultants to teachers in specific areas.
_____ Develop supplemental teaching/instructional materials.
_____ Offer summer training courses to teachers as well as new employees.
_____ Host teachers for summer employment in specific curriculum-related jobs.
_____ Assist teachers as volunteer aides (e.g., in health screening, grading papers, playground, etc.).

FOR THE SCHOOL

_____ Donate surplus equipment or supplies for classroom/office use.
_____ Provide meeting space or special facility use at our workplace.

Partnerships

_____Sponsor school contests and serve as judges (e.g., of writing, spelling, reading, etc.).
_____Participate in school beautification, repair, and renovation projects.
_____Assist with after-school activities (e.g., plays, athletics, band, etc.).
_____Help with fundraising activities (e.g., sales, events, drives, etc.).
_____Sponsor or organize a school club (e.g., math, computers, photography, etc.).
_____Assist in the production and publication of the school newspaper and yearbook.
_____Provide volunteer help in non-classroom settings (e.g., office, cafeteria, library, etc.).

Source: National Community Education Day Packet

Exhibit 6. School activities that benefit business

1. Display student work at your adopted business.
2. Entertain employees on special occasions by song, music, or dance.
3. Promote the produce of the adopter through word of mouth or literature about the business.
4. Do special art projects to promote any special sales or events of the adopter.
5. A classroom might adopt a certain department of the business and do special favors for those employees.
6. Support any outside activity of the business.
7. Do volunteer work at the business.
8. Present business with an appreciation certificate.
9. Have a tea or coffee honoring the adopted business.
10. Write a skit or song honoring the adopter.
11. Present to the business a key or spirit sticker from the adoptee.

Source: Rutherford County Board of Education
Murfreesboro, Tennessee

Partnerships

Exhibit 7. Samples of successful activities

The following activities were used successfully in adopt-a-school programs. Most required the students to exercise one or more of the basic skills.

1. **Field trips.** One adopter organized a visit to the company's plant. Prior to visiting the plant, the company gave the students a list of questions to ask employees. The students interviewed the employees on the job and wrote up the results. Later, they filled out applications for jobs.

2. **Public relations.** Students formed a public relations agency. They wrote information about the adopt-a-school program as press releases (they were give only 15 minutes for each assignment). The students also wrote a high school newsletter.

3. **Media.** Students in many schools produced school newspapers and in-house television programs featuring interviews of people from the adopting organization. Several adopting organizations also helped students develop school newspapers from scratch.

4. **Mini-internships.** Students spent time at business and professional offices studying employees on the job.

5. **Personnel.** Students were taken through employment procedures, including filling in applications and being interviewed. These programs generally focused on the importance of correctly written and spoken English.

6. **Incentive programs.** These included awards for attendance and achievement and various contests with company participants serving as role models for students and providing leadership training.

7. **Tutoring.** Tutoring programs ranged from remedial work on basic skills to guidance in science fair projects.

8. **Technical training.** Organizations offered training in accounting, bookkeeping, use of the computer, and model building.

9. **Research projects.** Projects included field work in business and manufacturing organizations, market research, library research on academic projects, and scientific report writing.

10. **Community awareness and service.** Organizations provided opportunities for students to learn to poll the community on public issues.

Exhibits

11. **Career guidance.** Organizations introduced students to different occupations and careers, emphasizing the skills required for entry into and success in the fields.

12. **Reading and math programs.** These programs met the student needs most often identified by the schools.

13. **Science and health programs.** These included preventative medicine, first aid, rudimentary diagnosis, sports medicine, supplementary science programs, and laboratory experiences.

14. **After-school programs.** These included a variety of academic and cultural activities which were often used as a reward for academic achievement and appropriate school behavior during the school day.

15. **Training programs.** Some companies offered their in-house training programs to high school students.

16. **Cultural programs.** Students were taken to various cultural institutions and events. They were required to do preliminary work and written assignments as follow-up.

17. **Counseling.** Organizations offered counseling for potential dropouts, children with emotional or school-learning problems, and pregnant students.

18. **Opportunities for teachers.** Organizations provided the following opportunities for teachers:

    a. Participation in the company's management training seminars
    b. Employment during summer months to update information and skills in business areas related to teaching and counseling
    c. In-service for teachers and invitations to the company to familiarize them with the organization's activities.

Source: Chicago Public Schools
Chicago, Illinois

Partnerships

Exhibit 8. School needs assessment form

Our school is participating in the adopt-a-school program, having been adopted by _____.

Now, we need to plan activities for our adoption. The logical starting point is with our needs. What "needs" within our school, or your classroom, could be addressed with the help of people from our adopter? (Remember, the emphasis in on their involvement, not their financial support.) What new, exciting thing might be done, that may or may not relate to needs?

Please complete this form, indicating needs/opportunities you think are appropriate topics for activities. If you have specific projects, share them, also.

There is an adopt-a-school procedure manual, which contains samples of others' successful activities, available in the principal's office. If you wish to come by and look at it, it may give you some ideas or get your own thoughts going.

When you have completed the form, return it to the office.

NAME _____

PHONE NUMBER _____

POSITION _____
(Teacher - subject/grade level, Parent, Student Council member)

School Needs _____

_____

_____

Specific Classroom Needs _____

_____

Opportunities for New Activities _____

_____

_____

Exhibits

Project Ideas _____

_____

_____

Source: Rutherford County Board of Education
Murfreesboro, Tennessee

Partnerships

Exhibit 9. Business/community volunteer interest form

Our company has volunteered to participate in the adopt-a-school program, and has chosen to "adopt" _____.

This program is an effort to make available to our school employees from our company/organization who can serve as role models and exemplify the positive benefits of education and the free enterprise system. More specifically, there are many opportunities for us to work with students on school projects, regular studies, and any activities which we can plan together.

There is an adopt-a-school procedure manual, which contains examples of others' successful activities, available in _____ office. If you wish to come by and look at it, it may give you some ideas or get your own thoughts going.

We are excited about our participation in this program, and are offering employees opportunities to indicate their interest in supporting this worthwhile community/school endeavor.

When you have completed the form, please return it to _____ by _____.

NAME _____ PHONE NUMBER _____

POSITION _____
(Job Title, Department, Shift)

_____ Tutoring of gifted students and those that are struggling _____ (subject)
_____ Assisting students in preparing school publications
_____ Workshops on economic issues for teachers
_____ Career awareness events
_____ Science and math action learning programs
_____ Sharing hobbies in and out of the classroom _____
_____ Teacher support in classroom, library helper, field trip chaperone, paper grader, etc. (specify) _____
_____ Sponsor for school club
_____ Help with incentive awards for achievement, attendance
_____ Act as judge for school event
_____ Other (specify) _____

Source: Rutherford County Board of Education
Murfreesboro, Tennessee

Exhibit 10. Sample partnership council organizational chart

ATLANTA PARTNERSHIP OF BUSINESS & EDUCATION

Executive Committee Officers, Exec. Director Superintendent of Schools	
Board of Directors	
Task Forces	
PARTNERS	

ATLANTA COUNCIL PTAs

- President and Vice President of Council
- Executive Committee
- Presidents of Local Schools PTA/PTSAs

RELIGIOUS COMMUNITY PARTNERSHIP

- Metro Atlanta Christian Council
- Joint Urban Ministries
- Ecumenical Community Ministries
- National Conference of Christians & Jews
- Individual Congregations

SUPERINTENDENT/ DEANS BREAKFAST CLUB

- Superintendent of Atlanta Public Schools
- Deans Local Colleges/ Schools of Education

Source: Atlanta Public Schools
Atlanta, Georgia

Partnerships

Exhibit 11. A large city's partnership plan

START-UP ORGANIZATION CHART
FOR THE PARTNERSHIP

Initial Business Interest	Desire to form a partnership
Greater Baltimore Committee (GBC)	Provide follow-up, technical assistance work to Baltimore City Public Schools
Baltimore City Public Schools (BCPS)	Work with business and GBC to identify needs, initiate selection of school, consider type, proximity, and student population.
School Selection	BCPS, GBC, and business set up interviews with principals. Preliminary needs assessment. Identify areas where business can assist.
Partnership Established	School selected. CEO and principal endorse partnership. Planning begins.

*This model is adaptable for single business/school partnerships as well as joint targeted partnerships.

Exhibits

PLANNING RESPONSIBILITIES CHART

Partnership Established

Commitment made. CEO welcomes partner and pledges donation of business' human resources.

Principal endorses partnership. Staff and teachers begin working on specific areas of need.

The Pledge

Formal agreement: Business and school write certificate for posting in business office announcing partnership. Tour of business for school staff.

Formal agreement: School and business write certificate for posting in school announcing partnership. School staff conducts tour of school for business representatives.

Designate Coordinators

CEO selects high-ranking representative to coordinate activities. Reports to CEO and has authority to allocate resources and arrange release time for volunteers.

Principal selects coordinator. Possibilities: principal, assistant principal, department head, teacher.

Assess Needs

Community outreach and commitment to education. Volunteers serve as instruction and administrative aides. Strengthen interpersonal skills of employees.

Students need role models, job skills, curriculum enhancement, incentives for achievement.

Establish Goals and Objectives

Build on commitment: Commit human resources and time to spark interest in students. Establish goals.

Address a specific problem, raise a proficiency level, foster career awareness. Plan activities.

KEY:

Business

School

Partnerships

Write Plan — **Written plan completed. Volunteer will visit school regularly to illustrate world of work, subject areas, and skills.**

Students and teachers will be exposed to various "jobs" and skills regularly. School will generate ideas for activities with business.

Recruit and Orient Volunteers — **Line up volunteers: Discuss program. Involve occupations.**

Teachers and staff prepare for activities. Involve parents.

KEY: **Business**

School

Exhibits

PARTNERSHIP ACTIVITIES CHART

Build/
Promote

Start small. Build program. Make company aware of the partnership. Inform employees.

Start small. Build program. Inform and involve student population, school staff, parents, and community.

Conduct
Activities

Regular visits begin. Guest speakers, worksite visits, incentives for attendance, non-instructional activities.

Work with volunteers. Facilitate volunteer visits—room assignments, materials, scheduling, etc.

Communicate/
Monitor

Communicate weekly with school coordinator. Address problems and concerns as they arise.

Communicate weekly with school coordinator. Address problems and concerns as they arise.

Evaluate

Continuing process: Have goals been achieved? Are activities worthwhile? Do employees enjoy and want to be involved? Can we do more?

Continuing Process: Have goals been achieved? Are activities worthwhile? Do students profit from volunteer activities? Can we do more?

KEY: **Business**
       Schools

Source: Baltimore City Schools
Baltimore, Maryland

Partnerships

Exhibit 12. A student banking program

PROGRAM	AGE OF STUDENTS	DESCRIPTION OF PROGRAM	BANK'S POSITION ON PROGRAM
Project STEP The Bank's Skills Training Educational Program	High school seniors and adults	70 job training classes in 17 skill areas taught by bank employees in bank equipment and training materials.	Bank supports Project STEP as the most beneficial educational program for recruiting purposes. Teachers recommend best students for employment. Recruiters contact recommended students and set up interviews. Other students apply at bank in regular way. Over 2,000 students are trained each year in STEP classes.
Regional Occupational Program (ROP)	High school usually seniors and adults	Students come into banking offices for on-the-job training from classes sponsored by Regional Occupational Programs. Students come from bank teller and banking occupational classes.	Bank has supported this program for nearly a decade as an excellent source of new hires for the banking office systems who have already had on-the-job training. Nearly 200 banking offices trained over 600 ROP students during the 1977-78 school year.
Exploratory Work Experience Education (EWEE)	High school students, usually younger than ROP students	Students explore banking careers in banking offices to see if banking interests them as a career.	General support; however, since students are usually younger, not as good a source of potential employees. Banking offices usually prefer ROP. During the 1977-78 school year, 99 EWEE students explored 43 bank offices.
General Work Experience Education (work experience)	High school students with work permits	Students work part-time for the bank and receive school credit or work experience.	Some support. Good source of part-time help in banking offices. During 1977-78 school year, 31 students were hired part-time in 22 banking offices.

Exhibits

College & University Internships	College & university students	Usually nonpaid programs designed around special research projects developed to meet the needs of the students and the bank.	Some support. Internships have been granted to exceptional students the bank would ultimately like to employ. Number of students is minimal and scattered throughout bank.
Cooperative Education	Community college and university students. Also can be full-time bank employees going to college at night and receiving credit for work experience.	Some paid work experience programs. Some nonpaid internship programs.	Little support. Bank's major commitment is toward programs which prepare students for entry-level jobs. During 1977-78 school year, 12 cooperative students were trained in 8 banking offices.
CETA (Comprehensive Employment Training Act)	High school students and adults	Programs vary depending on age of students and purpose. Usually, bank provides training and CETA pays students while they learn. It is hoped the bank will hire students upon completion of program.	No support except on individual basis. Bank has participated in CETA programs in the past with little success. Prefers other programs to this one due to success potential of students.

Source: Security Pacific Bank
Los Angeles, California

Partnerships
Exhibit 13. How a school helped a business

Services Provided by the School District to Honeywell

CAREER DEVELOPMENT
Wayne Bengtson conducted 12 half-day on-site career development seminars for MAvD personnel during the summer of 1984. These seminars, initiated in 1983, are to be continued in 1985 with 20 half-day sessions planned.

EFFECTIVE LISTENING SKILLS
Six sessions of "Effective Listening Skills" were conducted by Bob Erickson for MAvD personnel at Opus. This course, too, was initiated in 1984 and is to continue in 1985.

INTERVIEWING SKILLS
Following training with a consulting firm (provided by Honeywell), Career Counselor Jim Wolff tailored this course to satisfy MAvD needs. It was offered initially in November, 1984 for factor supervisors and is to be repeated at least twice in 1985.

WORD PROCESSING
Word processing/typing skills training is available and will be offered on an "as needed" basis.

FACILITIES USE
The School District's educational and recreational facilities (auditorium, gymnasiums, pools, athletic fields, film/video lab, etc.) are offered for use by MAvD. The high school complex and Central Community Center were utilized for Olympiad III, and various employee groups currently use some of the recreational facilities.

Exhibits

Joint Programs

SELF DEVELOPMENT SEMINARS
Four after-hours self-development seminars (two sponsored by MAvD and two by SLP) were offered for MAvD and SLP personnel as part of the ongoing Employee and Family Assistance Program. Dealing with anger, building self-esteem, loneliness/aloneness, and effective parenting.

Four SLP staff members (Anne Stokes, Ruth Hanson, Leigh Abrahamson, Pam Canning) conducted the four sessions on Effective Parenting. The first one dealt with pre-school aged kids, the second with elementary aged students. The second one included a presentation and discussion of learning styles. The third session was on adolescence and the fourth on abuse. This program will be offered during noon hour sessions in 1985-86.

VOLUNTEER TRAINING INSTITUTE
St. Louis Park Volunteer Coordinators are working with Honeywell staff to develop school and corporate training programs regarding, respectively, use of corporate volunteers and being a school volunteer.

Source: Honeywell, Inc., Publication on Partnership with Public Schools
St. Louis Park

Partnerships
Exhibit 14. Sample job descriptions for partners

The school coordinator

- Assists the principal and staff in identifying school needs.

- Initiates meetings of school staff, the adopter's coordinator, and adopt-a-school support staff to design programs to meet identified school needs.

- Completes and submits the school's action plan to the adopt-a-school central office.

- Arranges an orientation program for the adopter's resources staff prior to implementing the program in the school.

- Monitors evaluation of the adopt-a-school program and adjusts the program, if necessary, to better meet students needs.

- Plans meetings to ensure staff and community support of the program.

- Keeps the principal informed about the program.

The teacher

- Assists in designing an adopt-a-school program that meets school needs.

- Works in partnership with the adopter's resources staff in implementing the program in the classroom.

- Assists and supports the adopter's resources staff at all times in classroom presentation, demonstrations, and projects.

- Attends all presentations and participates in all activities.

- Works in partnership with the adopter's resources staff to bring student participation and interaction to the highest level.

- Evaluates and, if necessary, adjusts the adopt-a-school program to ensure quality.

- Keeps the school coordinator updated on the progress of the program.

- Attends all meetings regarding program operations and support.

Exhibits

The adopter's coordinator

- Assists in designing an adopt-a-school program which provides resources from the adopting organization to meet school needs.

- Initiates meetings with the school, the adopter, and the adopt-a-school support staff to discuss program design, implementation, and evaluation.

- Works with appropriate school staff to complete and submit and adopt-a-school action plan to the adopt-a-school central office for approval.

- Works with the school's staff to prepare and schedule an orientation session for the adopting organization's resources staff prior to their beginning the program in the school.

- Plans meetings within the organization to disseminate information about program operations and to encourage support.

The adopter's resources staff

- Assists in designing an adopt-a-school program, using the adopting organization's resources to meet identified school needs.

- Works in partnership with the adopt-a-school teacher in developing the program that will be implemented in the classroom.

- Determines with the adopt-a-school teacher program areas where student participation and interaction can be increased.

- Evaluates and, if necessary, adjusts the adopt-a-school program to maintain quality.

- Keeps the adopter's coordinator updated on program progress.

- Attends all meetings regarding program operations and support.

The adopt-a-school support staff

- Assists all newly adopted schools and all schools returning to adoption, as needed.

- Participates in the planning meetings between the adopter and the school, acting as a third party to clarify issues between the partners.

Partnerships

- Ensures that an action plan for the program is completed, agreed upon, and forwarded to the director of the adopt-a-school program for approval before implementation.

- Maintains contact, as needed, with the adopter's representatives and the school to ensure that the planned program is being implemented in a timely manner; assists in discussions regarding program modification, when necessary.

- Keeps the adopt-a-school central office informed about the program's activities and recommends solutions to any problems that may arise.

- Serves as a liaison person between the adopt-a-school central office and the adopting organization.

                    Source: Chicago Public Schools
                    Chicago, Illinois

Exhibit 15. Sample volunteer interview form

VOLUNTEER'S NAME   Miss
                                     Mr. _____
                                     Mrs.

_____
Street No. and Name

_____
City, State   Zip Code   Phone

Do you have any special qualifications or training? _____

_____

_____

Interests, skills, hobbies _____

_____

What age child do you feel most comfortable with? _____

Do you feel more comfortable working one-to-one or in the classroom? _____

_____

Type of school volunteer service preferred _____

_____

Available for School Volunteer Service

	MON.	TUES.	WED.	THURS.	FRI.
Morning					
Afternoon					
Evening					

Source: Los Angeles City Unified School District
Los Angeles, California

Partnerships

Exhibit 16. Sample corporate volunteer application form

Dr.
Mr.
Mrs.
Miss _____

Home Address _____
                    Street,   City,   State   Zip

Home Telephone _____

Job Title _____ Department _____

Employee No. _____ Business Phone _____

Do you speak a foreign language? YES_____ NO_____
If "Yes," identify the language(s) you speak _____

Please select your first and second choices of the day of the week and indicate your time preference that you would like to volunteer:

Mon. _____ Tues. _____ Wed. _____ Thurs. _____

Time _____ Time _____ Time _____ Time _____

Areas of Service

Academic
- ☐ English Tutor
- ☐ English as a Second Language
- ☐ Math Tutor
- ☐ Bookkeeping & Accounting
- ☐ Business Math
- ☐ Algebra
- ☐ Calculus
- ☐ General Math
- ☐ Geometry
- ☐ Trigonometry
- ☐ Reading Tutor
- ☐ Science Tutor
- ☐ Cosmetology (Grooming/Health/Hygiene)
- ☐ Creating Writing/Journalism
- ☐ Other _____
- ☐ Other _____

Vocational
- ☐ Applying for a Position (Interviews, Tests, Resume Preparation)
- ☐ Auto Mechanics
- ☐ Computer Technology and Data Processing
- ☐ Aeronautical Engineering
- ☐ Electrical Engineering
- ☐ Mechanical Engineering
- ☐ Secretarial Sciences
- ☐ Other _____
- ☐ Other _____

Source: Dade County Public Schools
Dade County, Florida

Exhibit 17. Sample volunteer orientation program

I. **Welcome and Introduction**

    A. Volunteer Personnel
    B. School Personnel

II. **Philosophy of Volunteering**

III. **History, Purpose, and Objectives of the Program and Its Role in the Community**

IV. **Administration**

    A. Channels of Communications

    B. School Policies

        1. Dress and behavior
        2. Health exam requirements
        3. Liability (insurance)
        4. Fund raising
        5. Discipline
        6. Releasing children to adults
        7. Visitors
        8. Students leaving classroom
        9. Teachers leaving classroom
        10. Books sent home
        11. Notes and letters sent home
        12. Lost and found
        13. Emergency calls during school hours and use of phone
        14. Use of custodial services
        15. Working in child's classroom
        16. Parking
        17. Teachers' lounge

V. **Volunteers**

    A. Responsibilities

        1. Conviction that what you are doing is right
        2. Interest in helping a child
        3. Dependability

Partnerships

    4. Loyalty
    5. Willingness to learn and accept supervision
    6. Confidentiality
       a. staff
       b. child
       c. school records

                Source: Dade County Public Schools
                      Dade County, Florida

Exhibit 18. Sample public relations plan

Good public relations plays a major role in the success of any program. One way of establishing good public relations for an adopt-a-school program is through publicity within the school system and the community.

1. **School System.** It is important that adopt-a-school activities and events be publicized within the school system. The school coordinator should submit photographs and stories of program activities and events to the adopt-a-school central office and to school publications. These articles will be considered for publication in Spotlight, the adopt-a-school newsletter, which is distributed to approximately 10,000 businesses, all schools, all adopters, and the media.

2. **Adopting Organization.** The adopting organization's coordinator should submit photographs and stories to his/her company publication to disseminate information about the program within the company. Whenever the publication prints a story about the program, the business coordinator should send copies to the school coordinator and to the adopt-a-school central office.

3. **News Media.** The adopt-a-school program has enjoyed good media coverage. Frequently, reporters contact the adopt-a-school central office for information. Articles submitted to the office are made available to these reporters.

Source: Chicago Public Schools
Chicago, Illinois

Partnerships

Exhibit 19. Evaluation questions

The following questions should be kept in mind in evaluating an adopt-a-school program:
1. Did the partners establish clearly stated objectives consistent with identified school needs?
2. Were the objectives related directly to the school's curriculum or were they concerned with enrichment on extracurricular activities?
3. Did the objectives contain a clear academic focus (reading, writing, math, science)?
4. Did the partners accomplish their objectives?
5. Did the program include varied, creative, and innovative activities and/or materials?
6. How many students were involved?
7. How much time (hours) did the adopting organization spend with the program?
8. How frequently did the adopter's staff meet with the students?
9. How many weeks was the program in operation with actual student participation?
10. Was the program conducted by the adopter on organization time or on personal time?
11. Did the adopting organization use resources other than its own, i.e., films, resource persons, journals, etc.?
12. Were school personnel other than the program teacher involved, i.e., counselors, the principal, etc.?
13. Is there documented evidence of the program's impact on the improvement of student reading, writing, math, attendance, etc.?
14. Did the adopting organization's program encourage similar organizations to participate in the adopt-a-school program?

Source: Chicago Public Schools
Chicago, Illinois

Exhibit 20. Evaluation form for school staff

Circle one number on each question.

Key: 1 - Poor; 2 - Average; 3 - Excellent; NA - Not Applicable

1. Did our company continuously help your school throughout the entire year?	1	2	3	NA
2. Was our company available to help when called upon to do so?	1	2	3	NA
3. Was our adopt-a-school chairman friendly and eager to help?	1	2	3	NA
4. Was it helpful to you to have our company sponsoring you?	1	2	3	NA
5. Did the service of our company to the students of your school benefit them?	1	2	3	NA
6. Overall, how would you rate our company's performance in the adopt-a-school program?	1	2	3	NA

How would you improve the program for the next school year? _____

_____

_____

_____

_____

Source: Rutherford County Board of Education
Murfreesboro, Tennessee

Partnerships

Exhibit 21. Evaluation form for corporate staff

Circle one number on each question.

Key: 1 - Poor; 2 - Average; 3 - Excellent; NA - Not Applicable

1. Was the publicity of the adopt-a-school program suitable to your company?	1	2	3	NA
2. Did our school use the program and what your company offered to the fullest potential?	1	2	3	NA
3. Was our adopt-a-school chairman friendly and easy to work with?	1	2	3	NA
4. Did the employees of your company back the adopt-a-school program?	1	2	3	NA
5. Did you feel you benefit our school?	1	2	3	NA
6. Overall, how would you rate the adopt-a-school program in general?	1	2	3	NA

How would you improve the program for the next school year? _____

_____

_____

_____

_____

Source: Rutherford County Board of Education
Murfreesboro, Tennessee

Acknowledgments

The American Association of School Administrators (AASA) would like to thank all those who made this publication possible. We especially appreciate the input from those who responded to our survey about partnerships in their school-community, sharing not only descriptive material but also evaluations of what worked and what did not. Anne Lewis, currently a Washington, D.C., based free-lance writer and former editor of Education USA and recent president of the Education Writers Association, sorted through the hundreds of replies and researched other sources to produce the basic manuscript.

We would also like to thank T. Susan Hill and Debbie Demmon-Berger, manager and senior editor of The BUSINESS SERVICE NETWORK, for their fine editing and production of the finished book.

Several members of the AASA staff contributed to this publication. Joanne Kaldy, managing editor, provided some editing. Anne Dees, publications manager, and Gary Marx, associate executive director, served as project directors.

AASA commends the efforts of all contributors as reflective of the cooperative spirit behind the many successful school/community partnerships reported here.